ANUNNAKI ORIGINS
THE EPIC OF CREATION
NEW STANDARD ZUIST EDITION

POCKET EDITION

Published from
Mardukite Borsippa HQ, San Luis Valley, Colorado
Founding Church of Mardukite Zuism,
Mardukite Academy & Systemology Society
for religious and educational purposes only.

ANUNNAKI ORIGINS

THE EPIC OF CREATION

NEW STANDARD ZUIST EDITION

Developed by Joshua Free for the
Church of Mardukite Zuism

THE JOSHUA FREE IMPRINT
JFI PUBLICATIONS

© 2023, JOSHUA FREE

ISBN : 978-1-961-50902-3

A special pocket version of
Babylonian Magic (Liber-E)
first published in 2011
as "Magan Magic" and
edited for founding the
Church of Mardukite Zuism

Pocket Paperback Edition — *June 2023*

Also available in hardcover as
"Babylonian Myth & Magic"

mardukite.com

The _Original_ Mystical Teachings of Planet Earth

Long-lost secrets of ancient Mesopotamian magic and Babylonian mysticism drawn from cuneiform tablets are revealed to all in this special pocket paperback edition of the Mardukite guide to esoteric archaeological understanding of the Enuma Elis tablet series, which served as the basis for later creation stories and even the "Book of Genesis."

Even if you think you already know all about Babylonian Magic and Sumerian Star-Gates...

Here is a Master Key to the ancient mystic arts; true knowledge concerning the power of creation and manifestation in this Universe -- and the Anunnaki entities that these arts are dedicated to. Their spirit remains strongly alive with us today.

Here is the New Standard Zuist Edition of the classic text by world renowned Joshua Free; a pocket paperback version of the original "Babylonian Magic" (Liber-E) discourse (first published as "Magan Magic" in 2011) edited for the Church of Mardukite Zuism. This volume redefines our understanding of the "Chaldean Genesis" or "Epic of Creation" and establishes stronger foundations for revival interest in Babylonian mysticism and the Anunnaki spiritual tradition of Mesopotamia, which influenced innumerable cultures and the development of human civilization thereafter.

New Standard Zuist Editions:

Anunnaki Bible – The Cuneiform Scriptures
Anunnaki Gods – The Sumerian Religion
Anunnaki History – The Magic of Babylon
Anunnaki Origins – The Epic of Creation
Anunnaki Rites – The Maqlu Ritual Book
What is Mardukite Zuism – The Power of Zu

TABLET OF CONTENTS

10TH ANNIVERSARY INTRODUCTION

by Joshua Free

The Mardukite Chamberlains (Mardukite Research Organization) completed its Year-1 cycle of work in early 2010—and those efforts culminated into an anthology first released as *"Necronomicon: The Anunnaki Bible"*—but which, for a recent solidification of our tradition as Mardukite Zuism, has also been published as *"The Complete Anunnaki Bible"*; and even a newly revised pocket-portable abridged format, *"Anunnaki Bible: The Cuneiform Scriptures (New Standard Zuist Edition),"* is available. That culmination of material has certainly earned its recognition as a critical staple and source book for a modern Mardukite revival, even now, over a decade later.

Although a necessary foundation to work from, completion of the Year-1 (2009) work proved to be only a beginning for the route that would carry and build a global underground spiritual movement, now, into the 2020's and beyond with a revitalized "religious brand" as *Mardukite Zuism* and its very effective *Systemology* of applied spiritual technology. Much of this would not have been possible—or even coherently relevant—were it not for the pivotal Year-2 (2010) continuation of efforts made by "Chamberlains Alumni," those that dedicated another year of attention to the practical esoteric interpretation of the "*Anunnaki Bible*" and its background.

In 2010, the "Mardukite Chamberlains" began publishing an esoteric history series by Joshua Free, establishing stronger foundations for the modern revival interest. This included "Liber-50" (released as "*Sumerian Religion*" and "*The Gates of the Necronomicon*"), "Liber-W" ("*The Book of Marduk by Nabu*") and "Liber-M" ("*Maqlu Ritual Book*")—all of which have been reissued as 10th Anniversary Collector's Hardcovers. "Liber-50" is also available as "*Anunnaki Gods: The Sumerian Religion*" (New Standard Zuist Edition). "Liber-M" is also available as "*Anunnaki Rites: The Maqlu Ritual Book*" (New Standard Zuist Edition).

However, the actual series conclusion appeared in 2011, with "Liber-51" and "Liber-E"—which were combined and reissued in a 10th Anniversary collector's edition hardcover as "*Babylonian Myth & Magic.*" And the second portion of this—"Liber-E"—finally appears in this *New Standard Zuist Edition* (that you now hold) as a stand-alone title for the first time since an original issue as "*Magan Magic.*" The first portion (Liber-51) is also available in the present pocket paperback series as "*Anunnaki History: The Magic of Babylon.*"

10TH ANNIVERSARY FOREWORD

"The Gates-Games of Marduk"
by David Zibert

The esoteric concept of *"Gates"*—*Gateways* or *Star-Gates*—is a central theme in Babylonian lore and its later derivatives. Oftentimes, these are symbolically interpreted by "mystics" and "magicians" as *Thresholds* connecting between alternate (or parallel) "dimensions," "planes" or "realities."

During most occult initiation processes, the *Seeker* is guided through a series of specific dramatic ceremonial enactments in the Physical Universe that are intended to correlate with a Spiritual Universe, as per the famous Hermetic doctrine of "AS ABOVE, SO BELOW,"[1] leading an initiate through a kind of labyrinthine spiritual/mind maze —a "game" whereby the magician or priest seeks Ascension by moving through such symbolic *Gateways* and *Tunnels*.[2] These types of "games" are often referred to as "Magickal Pathworking"

---

1   While famously attributed to Hermes Trismegistus, this quote is originally found on an older Babylonian *cuneiform* tablet; see *"Tablets of Destiny (Revelation)"* (*Liber-One*) by Joshua Free.

2   Different semantics exist for the concept of *Gates* (described here) in every ancient culture across the globe. These may be readily and easily researched, if the *Seeker* is so inclined.

or *Gatewalking*. Such a concept, in one form or another, will undoubtedly be already familiar to those acquainted with the occult underground; yet many times, a modern practitioner is likely to overlook the actual nature and significance of these *Gates*.

Sure enough, the very use of "*Gate*" semantics—*Thresholds*, *Portals* or any kind of *Door*—to represent another dimension or reality, is merely a *symbol* for the mind (or control center) to process data from a higher frequency of *Beingness*—the data coming from the *other side* of the *Gate*—down to the physical (*beta*) reality. A *symbol* is never the "thing" symbolized. The *symbol* is a *symbol*; and that is all there is to it.

> *Symbols* are frequently misunderstood
> *to be* equal to that which they represent.

So, this begs-the-question: Why exactly are practitioners using semantics and symbols of *Gates* in the first place? What is a *Gate*? A kind of *doorway*? Okay, what then about that?Perhaps a "door" is a type of intermediary *opening* between two different places or points in space...maybe? That seems rather legit if looking at and considering a bit of the aforementioned "games" and how they work—and these can get pretty involved; and there's nothing wrong with that. *Except for one point*: that's not actually what a "door" is at all!

And those beings—those who designed the rules of this "game" are taking great care that everyone is too distracted by the systems to notice that. They are, in fact, counting on this to keep the "game" alive. Simply stated:

> A *"door"* is a willfully built and directed *opening* through a willfully built and directed *barrier.*

That's all there is to *that*. Now, apply *that* to the "games" being played out in this universe, and realize how someone, somewhere, has intentionally put those barriers up, making you believe that he's some kind of authority over yourself, the real Self, and that you absolutely have to move through some maze like a mouse to see the Light at the end of the tunnel, when all you have to do is simply take back responsibility for playing the "game" and remove these barriers you were enforced to be in agreement with; to actually meet-up with your true Self and realize that in the holistic nature of spiritual (*Alpha*)[3] existence, that the "Clear Light" was there all along. *Do you see that?*

---

3   Semantics of "Alpha" and "Beta" existence and "control centers" are derived from "*Mardukite Systemology*" materials; "*Mardukite Zuism: A Brief Introduction*" is found in this present book.

* * * * * * *

The way the "game" of physical (*beta*) reality is set up is demonstrated in the Babylonian *Epic of Creation*—the *Enuma Eliš*—where MARDUK endeavored to order the physical (*beta*) universe/reality through what is described as the fashioning and sealing of *Gates*. The famous *Epic* relates how control over the game of reality is somehow bound to the control of some nebulous "*Tablets of Destiny*," which, in the beginning, are in possession of TIAMAT.

The *Enuma Eliš* is not only the Archetypal *Epic of Creation*, it's also the Archetypal "*Fantasy Adventure*" where a hero goes to slay an evil dragon in order to retrieve a magical treasure. TIAMAT is the "evil one" in this instance, but more accurately, she has the *Tablets of Destiny*—and MARDUK succeeded in convincing his fellow *Anunnaki* to agree for him to direct his attention toward being the maker of the rules, the setter of barriers—the "*Game-Master.*" In view of the *Epic*: should MARDUK succeed in slaying the dragon, he is promised to have ultimate authority over creation, bypassing the Cosmic Law of causality by somehow getting the other *Anunnaki*—and then later on, *Humanity*—to willfully agree to said authority; the very way to make up the rules...

"The ANUNNAKI told MARDUK:
Thy fate is unequaled, thy word is ANU.
Your words shall be command,
In your power shall it be to exalt and to
  abase.
None among the gods shall transgress your
  boundary."

—*"Enuma Eliš,"* Tablet-IV

"The ANUNNAKI set out a garment
And continued to speak to MARDUK.
'May thy fate, O lord, be supreme among
  the gods,
To destroy and to create; speak only the
  word,
And your command shall be fulfilled.
Command now that the garment vanish;
Speak the word again and let the garment
  reappear!'
Then he spake the words and the garment
  vanished;
Again he commanded it and the garment
  reappeared."

—*"Enuma Eliš,"* Tablet-IV

Even before engaging KINGU and TIAMAT in
battle, it is seen that the powers of MARDUK
come first from his own *Self-Determinism* to act—
and be at *Cause*—in the political-play of the

"*gods.*" MARDUK is described as the *only* member of the *Anunnaki* willing to take any *Responsibility* in this matter. By doing so, he directs his *Will* "against all odds" in a grand attempt to become the rule-maker of the "game":

> "All the *gods* have turned to [TIAMAT], with those, whom you created,
> They go to her side. I sent ANU,
>   but he could not withstand her;
> NUDIMMUD⁴ was afraid and turned back.
> But MARDUK has set out, the champion of the gods, your son;
> To set out against TIAMAT his heart has called him."
>
> —"*Enuma Eliš,*" Tablet-III

> "If I [MARDUK], your avenger,
> Conquer TIAMAT and give you life, [...]
> With my word in place, I will decree fate.
> May whatsoever I do remain unaltered,
> May the word of my lips never be changed nor made to no avail."
>
> —"*Enuma Eliš,*" Tablet-III

---

4   An alternate name for ENKI, meaning "*The Fashioner.*"

Now I hope this won't be a spoiler for newcomers, but MARDUK does successfully gain control of the *Tablets of Destiny,* simultaneously killing TIAMAT and her brood. MARDUK's overtaking of physical reality is clear as TIAMAT loses touch with the consensual reality that she just previously had dominion over, the tablets stating: "[…] she acted possessed and lost her sense of reason." The remainder of the *Epic* describes how MARDUK set up rules of his own by *"postulating"* a reality based on agreements about *"barriers,"* or else, *something to be free from*—pretty carceral[5] stuff alright: the *Gates* system—or *Matrix*—underlying physical (*beta*) reality to this day. But, MARDUK is a clever fellow—and, of course, he just left the *Key* to the *Locks* around for us, in plain sight:

> "With the *Key* known only to my *Race.*
>   Let none enter that *Gate,*
> Since to invoke *Death* is to utter the final
>   prayer."
>
>   —*"Enuma Eliš,"* Tablet-VI

So while it might seem to some that the efforts of MARDUK relayed within the *Enuma Eliš* is what has entrapped humanity into this existence as some kind of "evil demiurge"—which is the view taken by the original "Gnostics" and their derivati-

---

5   *"Carceral"* – of, or pertaining to, a prison or imprisonment.

ves—it is not so. The Babylonian *Epic of Creation* is rather a gift of MARDUK to humanity. It contains the *Keys* of reality systematization and its engineering; how it is done, but also how it can be undone.

These *Arcane Tablets* composing the *Creation Epic* relate, quite simply, "*Creation*"—that is, something willfully and purposefully "made" by an *Awareness*. We are now able to clearly see the systematic pattern behind such Creation, then undo and redo it under full *Responsibility of Self*.

And that's what "Mardukite Systemology" *is*.

That is what is meant by "using ancient wisdom to unlock human potential."

MARDUK is thus the Archetypal *Alpha Spirit*[6] incarnated. Here is why it is said, in the celebrated Mardukite Incantation of Eridu: "It is not I, but MARDUK who commands the incantation." This method does not mean a surrendering of the Self to an outside force that is personified by a god-form. it is taking back contact with the real *Self*—

---

6   *"Alpha Spirit"* – a spiritual lifeform; the True
     Self or "I-AM"; the spirit that is controlling the
     physical body (genetic vehicle) using a Lifeline,
     or continuum, of spiritual "ZU" energy. Refer to
     "Mardukite Zuism: A Brief Introduction."

the *Alpha Self*—of which MARDUK is a demonstration of.

Actuality of the literal events in the tale itself becomes irrelevant; because a workable method of reaching higher realities has been drawn from it.

And what is workable *is* true.

The *Enuma Eliš* is not only the *Epic of Creation* for a Physical (*Beta*) Universe, but also the *creation of human ability* to reclaim Self. Everyone carries within Self the potential to be MARDUK. This means you and I, here and now, have the right to awaken this potential as it was foretold on these *Arcane Tablets*.

It has always been there.

All you have to do is *remember*.

S*pirit of the Earth, remember!*
Spirit of the Sky, remember!

~ David Zibert
Master Mardukite of Canada
Council of Nabu-Tutu
Systemology A.T. Lab Office, Québec
Summer Solstice 2021

MARDUKITE

ZUISM

A BRIEF
INTRODUCTION

*According to the most ancient
historical records
written at the birth of our
modern civilization...* *

432,000 YEARS AGO...*

a small population of advanced beings—called the <u>ANUNNAKI</u>—began developing the planet Earth for their purposes. These elite Self-Actualized spiritual beings resided on Earth in physical bodies, but found their forms inadequate for the physical labors required. Enter: the "Human Condition." Ancient "<u>cuneiform</u>" tablet writings from Sumerians and Babylonians of Mesopotamia are clear regarding the original creation and systematic programming of Humanity.

CUNEIFORM...

is the oldest known writing system used by scribes of ancient Babylon to record their wisdom and the history of humanity on <u>clay tablets</u>. "Cuneiform" is named for its style of wedge-shaped script formed by a <u>reed pen</u> called a "<u>stylus.</u>" Rather than an alphabet of letters, cuneiform is a system of "<u>signs</u>" representing "things" and "ideas." These may be combined to represent even more complex "signs."

---

* Version 1.1 – First published in 2019 as "*Mardukite Zuism: A Brief Introduction*" in booklet form.

Many concepts adopted for modern "<u>Mardukite Zuism</u>" are derived from cuneiform tablets. The ANUNNAKI introduced complex writing systems in order to program civilization and all parameters of Reality for the Human Condition. Legendary "<u>Tablets of Destiny</u>" (Divine Truth, supreme knowledge and cosmic power of the "gods") were first introduced to Humanity in the Babylonian narrative known best as the "<u>Epic of Creation</u>.

THE ARCANE TABLETS.

Ancient Babylonians used the Tablets of Destiny & Creation Epic to systematize all cosmic knowledge into a workable <u>paradigm</u> called "Mardukite Zuism"—a <u>systemology</u> received directly from the ANUNNAKI.

<u>Paradigm</u> : an all-encompassing standard or religion used to view the world and communicate reality.

<u>Systemology</u> : applied philosophies of Mardukite Zuism combined with personal spiritual techniques and technology ("Tech") that is effectively demonstrating systematic principles of a "paradigm."

THE EPIC OF CREATION.

Seven cuneiform tablets compose the ancient <u>Babylonian Epic of Creation</u>, named the <u>Enuma Eliš</u> by scholars after its opening lines. These seven tablets are the basis for what later traditions refer to as the *"Seven Days of Creation."* The *Epic of Creation* tablets describe development of all existences with a Divine artistic perfection. The Enuma Eliš is the core example of religious literature from Babylon, which served as the basis for ancient *"Mardukite Zuism"*—the first true systematized religion in history.

THE SYSTEMOLOGY OF LIFE, UNIVERSES & EVERYTHING.

The *Arcane Tablets* describe the division of the ALL by the LAW, outside of which is but INFINITY. The *Epic of Creation* describes these activities as "mythology."

The Mardukite Systemology "Standard Model" uses the same information to demonstrates...

that <u>ALL</u> ("AN-KI") envelops both:
the <u>Spiritual Existences</u> ("AN")
and the <u>Physical Existences</u> ("KI")
divided by <u>Cosmic Law</u> and
connected by <u>Life-Awareness</u> ("ZU")
and beyond which is only the <u>Abyss</u>,
an <u>Infinity of Nothingness</u> ("ABZU").

ANCIENT SUMERIAN DEFINITIONS.

<u>ABZU</u> = "Abyss" ("Nothingness")
<u>ZU</u> = "Spiritual Life" ("Awareness")
<u>ANKI</u> = "All Existences" ("Existence")
<u>AN</u> = "Spiritual Universe" ("Heaven")
<u>KI</u> = "Physical Universe" ("Earth")

ALTERNATE MARDUKITE NEXGEN
SYSTEMOLOGY DEFINITIONS.

<u>ABZU</u> = "Infinity of Nothingness"
<u>ZU</u> = "Awareness of Alpha Spirit"
<u>ANKI</u> = "The Standard Model"
<u>AN</u> = "Alpha Existence" ("Spiritual")
<u>KI</u> = "Beta Existence" ("Physical")

AN
ZU
KI
ABZU
(Infinity of Nothingness)
"THE ALL"
(Potential Everythingness)
"THE LAW"
(The Cosmos)
INFINITY
SPIRITUAL
(alpha)
PHYSICAL
(beta)

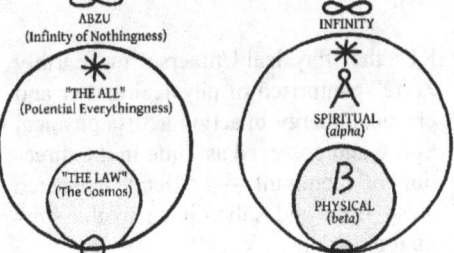

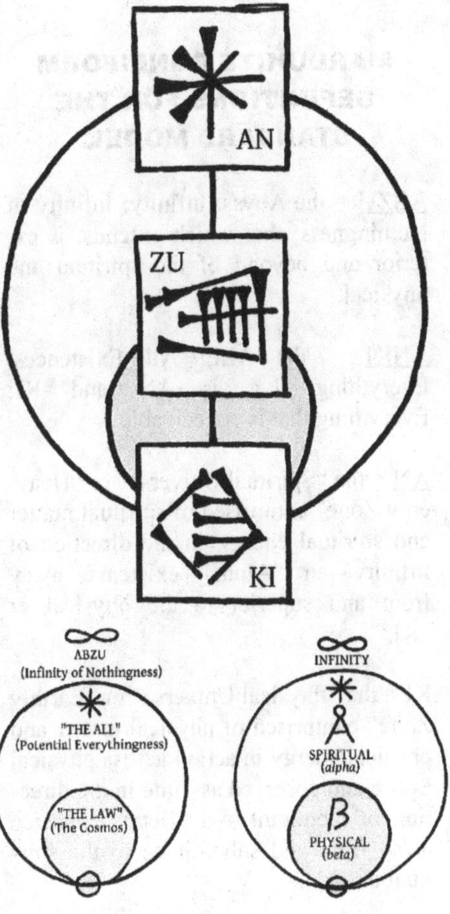

MARDUKITE CUNEIFORM DEFINITIONS FOR THE STANDARD MODEL.

<u>ABZU</u> = the Abyss; Infinity; Infinity of Nothingness; that which extends, is exterior and beyond of the spiritual and physical.

<u>ANKI</u> = the ALL; All Existences; Everything that is AN and KI; Everything that is conceivable.

<u>AN</u> = the "Spiritual Universe" or "Heavenly Zone" comprised of spiritual matter and spiritual energy, in the direction of Infinity—an "Alpha" existence away from and superior to the physical or "KI."

<u>KI</u> = the "Physical Universe" or "Earthly Zone" comprised of physical matter and physical energy in action across physical Space and observed as Time in the direction of Continuity—a "Beta" existence away from and subordinate to the spiritual or "AN."

<u>ZU</u> = "to know"; "knowingness"; "Awareness" or "consciousness"; spiritual energy and matter of AN that is observed as "Lifeforce" in KI; "Spiritual Life Energy"; the actual personal spiritual Identity or "Awareness" of Self as Spirit which extends along a "line" from the Spiritual Universe (AN) to the Physical Universe (KI).

THE TABLETS OF DESTINY & BABYLONIAN CREATION EPIC.

The Absolute behind ALL Existence is referred to on the *Tablets of Destiny* as the Infinity of Nothingness. It is the only constant static of latent unmanifest potentiality of ALL and Everythingness.

The LAW—Cosmic Law—is defined as the Cosmic Dragon—TIAMAT—on "Epic of Creation" Tablets. She is the First Cause or movement across a "Sea of Infinity." Later, the LAW becomes a division between Spiritual Existence ("AN") and any Physical Universe ("KI"). The LAW—Tiamat—permeating ALL, uses the *Tablets of Destiny* and then fixes the systems of finite potential: The Systems of Manifestation—Substance, Motion and Awareness.

"Before heaven or earth are named," the formation and interaction of active existences —"substances" and "bodies" and "Life" and "gods"—creates turbulence and waves of action through space. The governing system of Cosmic Law—Tiamat—responds accordingly. She fixes the Tablets of Destiny to her "deputy"—a messenger wave action of the LAW named "Kingu" and sends him rippling out to "meet" the Anunnaki "gods."

The Anunnaki Assembly of "gods" prepare to battle The LAW. When none among them comes forth to engage, it is the Anunnaki "god" MARDUK that volunteers as hero to confront Kingu and Tiamat—but with a condition that the Anunnaki Assembly recognize him as "Chief of the Gods" upon his success.

When MARDUK approaches the LAW directly, he is flanked by Kingu and the "army of Ancient Ones." MARDUK is able to relinquish the Tablets of Destiny from Kingu. With the Tablets of Destiny, Marduk conquers a true understanding of Cosmic Law and thereby Tiamat.

THE TABLETS OF DESTINY
& SELF-HONESTY.

Marduk uses the Tablets of Destiny to discover "Self-Honesty" and Divine Knowledge governing "Cosmic Ordering"—systems dividing the "Spiritual Universe" (AN) from a "Physical Universe" (KI). The two universes are connected only by a stream of Spiritual Lifeforce Awareness that Sumerians called ZU. Wisdom from the Arcane Tablets is later passed down to and concealed by an ancient esoteric secret society in Babylon: the Scribes, High Priests and Priestesses of Mardukite Zuism.

Self-Honesty is a term describing an original "Alpha" state of clear knowingness and Self-directed beingness. "Self-Honesty" is the most basic and true expression of Self as "I-AM"—free of artificial attachments; reactive-response conditioning; and imposed or enforced programming as Reality for the Human Condition. Spiritual development in modern *Mardukite Zuism* is referred to as the "Pathway to Self-Honesty" and the "Gateway to Infinity." It is modeled directly from the Ancient Mystery Tradition observed at the Temples of Babylon.

THE KEY TO THE GATE.

"I will take my Blood—and with Bone—I will fashion a Race of Humans to keep Watch of the Gate. And from the Blood of Kingu I will create another Race of Humans to inhabit the Earth in service to the Gods—so shrines to the Anunnaki may be built and the temples filled. I will bind the Elder Gods to the Watchtowers; let them keep watch over the Gate of Abzu and the Gate of Tiamat and Gate of Kingu—and with a Key that shall be ever hidden, known to none, except only to my Mardukites." —MARDUK, *Enuma Elis, Creation Tablet VI*.

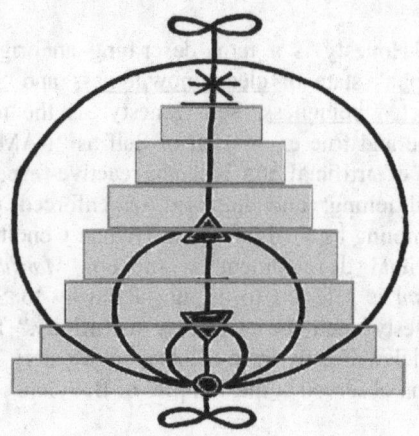

THE ANUNNAKI LADDER OF LIGHTS & BABYLONIAN GATEWAYS TO INFINITY.

ZIGGURAT TEMPLES in Babylonia—and throughout Mesopotamia—served to remind populations of the ZU connecting "Heaven" and "Earth."

Seven-stepped "levels" of the physical ZIG-GURAT TEMPLES of Babylonia—and seven corresponding Gates—represent spiritual levels of actualized Awareness; states of Self-purification (or "spiritual defragmentation") as they ascend in the direction of AN toward Infinity of Supreme Beingness—the Pathway of Self-Honesty—in imitation of the footsteps of the gods during their descent through the "spheres" or "Gates."

COSMOLOGY AND METAPHYSICS.

All Things in the Physical Universe are in motion—wave motions of "energy and matter in space measured as-and-across time." Continuity of the Physical Universe (KI) is divided by LAW and encompassed by the ALL (ANKI).

The direction of AN extends toward ABZU, an Infinity of Nothingness beyond effective existence.

The true <u>Alpha Self</u> is a source—the "spiritual cause" of "physical effects." It engages a <u>Self-determined WILL</u> from its "spiritual" <u>Alpha existence</u> to actualize Awareness for "physical" <u>Beta existence</u> experience as "Life."

USING ANCIENT WISDOM TO UNLOCK HUMAN POTENTIAL.

Communication of clear wisdom and true knowledge from Arcane Tablets is distorted as it passes through time and geography, diverse languages and authoritarian cultures using the "Power" to program the masses and fragment the Human Condition away from Self-Honesty.

Use of this ancient wisdom reveals the Keys to "<u>Cosmic Ordering</u>"—applying the highest Self-directed understanding of "cause-and-effect" sequences in the Physical Universe.

MARDUKITE ZUISM, SYSTEMOLOGY & SPIRITUALITY.

The Spiritual Universe (AN)—of metaphysical or spiritual energy and metaphysical or spiritual matter is not dependent on the Physical Universe (KI) to exist; the two are existentially independent of each other, maintaining a single channel, conduit or connection, which is <u>Alpha Spirit</u> "Awareness" as Spiritual Life or ZU. The Alpha Spirit engages a <u>ZU-line</u>, a spiritual life-line of ZU energy to a genetic vehicle or organic body to experience physical beta existence.

MARDUKITE ZUISM DEFINITIONS FOR SYSTEMOLOGY.

<u>ALPHA SPIRIT</u> = a spiritual lifeform; the True Self or "I-AM"; the spirit that is controlling the physical body or "genetic vehicle" using a Lifeline or continuum of spiritual "ZU" energy.

<u>ASCENSION</u> = actualized Awareness elevated to (AN) spiritual existence that is exterior to beta-existence.

<u>BETA-EXISTENCE</u> = manifestation in the Physical Universe (KI); the state of existence or condition of frequency specific to physical energy and physical matter in physical space.

<u>FRAGMENTATION</u> = breaking into parts; fractioning wholeness; fracture of holism; discontinuity; separation; outside the state of Self-Honesty.

<u>GENETIC VEHICLE</u> = a physical life-form; the physical (beta) body controlled by the (Alpha) Spirit using a continuous Lifeline of ZU energy.

<u>HUMAN CONDITION</u> = a default programmed conditioned state standard issue Human existence/experience.

<u>ZU-LINE</u> = a spectrum of Spiritual Life-Energy (ZU); an energetic channel or Identity-Continuum connecting Alpha Spirit Awareness from Infinity-to-Infinity including the full physical beta range.

THE HIGHEST FORM OF
TRUE DIVINE WORSHIP.

The true Destiny of Humanity is to achieve spiritual <u>Self-Actualization</u>; the reunion of Self with the Divine. Attaining Self-Honesty in this Life is the most important step a person can take toward achieving their highest ideals, goals and realizations.

The Highest form of "True Worship" begins with the Spirit—the true Self—and all external practices, rituals, ceremonies and historical examples are but outer reflections of this ideal. The Highest form of "Sin" is against the Spirit —against the Self—and its ability to maintain Self-Honesty. There are modes of thought, action and Self-direction of effort that will contribute toward Ascension; and modes that lead away from that.

Beta experiences of "Sin"—pain, fear, guilt, anger—are all related to personal fragmentation; and emotional turbulence from all of these may be released—and intention energy redirected— because: <u>we are all co-creators of Reality in this lifetime!</u>

SPHERES OF EXISTENCE, INFLUENCE & UTILITARIAN ETHICS OF SYSTEMOLOGY.

The prime directive of all beta existence is: *to exist*. The continuation of existence is the purpose behind all existence. Between realization of Self and Infinity, there are many spheres of existence that we may influence. All of the spheres are interconnected.

There is nothing in existence that is in absolute exclusion to all existence. Each sphere of existence supports subsequent existences and assists reaches toward higher spheres of influence.

The greatest good contributes to the greatest continuation of optimum existence for the greatest sphere of inclusion. Degrees of rightness and wrongness are determined by Cosmic Law and are reflected in the quality of, and continuation of, an optimal existence at the highest sphere of existence.

Individual happiness is attained via the channel to the highest sphere. Human unhappiness is the result of "selfishness" and/or lack of "spiritual Self-Actualization" and "Awareness."

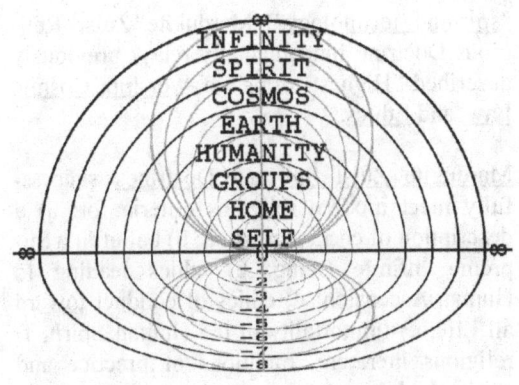

ZU : MARDUKITE ZUISM & MODERN ZUIST RELIGION.

History demonstrates how dangerous, troublesome and easily misused the concept of "RELIGION" is; so, for purposes of incorporating Mardukite Zuism as a contemporary standard, the idea of "religion" is here treated as:

a concise spiritual paradigm, set of beliefs and practices, regarding Divinity, Infinite Beingness—or else "God."

Mardukite Zuism operates under a premise of very specific beliefs and a "systemology" of "spiritual technology." Mardukite Zuist Religious Doctrine fundamentally relays previously described "Highest forms" of Worship, Cosmic Law, and Ethics.

Mardukite Zuist Spiritual Doctrines successfully meet modern religious criteria for: a) a description of cosmic creation; b) belief in a Supreme Infinite Being; c) ethics leading to Human Ascension; d) ethics of conduct toward all Life; e) Immortality of the Human Spirit; f) religious literature, traditions of practice and spiritual advisement.

GOALS & IDEALS OF MARDUKITE ZUISM.

The word "ZU" meant "knowing" in original Sumerian cuneiform script. Goals and ideals of Zuism reflect this. Mardukite Zuism seeks to assist an individual in reclaiming a realization of the True Self or "I-AM" as the Immortal Spirit, in line with a most ancient directive: to "Know Thyself."

In view of the fact that all modern humans are subjected to technologies depriving them of their freedoms to *be*, *think*, *know* and pursue truth: the goals and ideals of Zuism are to effectively revive and repair these very abilities and certainties of the Individual—as an increase of "Actualized Awareness."

INFINITY, "GOD" & SUPREME BEINGNESS

The Spiritual Philosophy of Zuism is systematized by a Standard Model. It demonstrates Absolute Supreme Beingness associated with the Highest realization of "God" as INFINITY. No thing is Higher or Absolute than the Infinity of Nothing—and reducing Supreme Beingness to any finite personality or character trait is to limit and defile with lesser "words."

The Highest Name of God cannot be conceived —hence our symbolic use of the Infinity Sign:

∞

...or Sumerian cuneiform word-sign: "ABZU"
—"The Infinite Nothingness and
Source of All ZU."

The Spiritual Universe (AN) is *All-as-One* because it exists as an infinite singularity or stasis:

infinite potential with no gradient or observed motion; which is its own continuity.

The Physical Universe (KI) is *All-as-One* because it is in continuous motion, with all manifest parts working systematically as a continuity of beta-existence.

A "spiritual continuum" or "conduit channel" of ZU—absolute energy from the Spiritual Universe (AN)—links our Awareness levels of "I-AM," "True Self" or Spirit ("Alpha Spirit") with the degrees of motion and variation in the Physical Universe.

This Alpha Spirit or "Soul" is the true Awareness, "I" or "Self" connected to the operation and control of the physical body.

THE TRUE HUMAN ALPHA SPIRIT.

The true Self is the "I" or "Spirit" regardless of its position, degree or level of Awareness. Spirit remains. Whatever "spiritual energy-matter" composes the Alpha Spirit or "soul"—it must occupy this "other space" with its spiritual existence and then project its Awareness and Will onto the Physical Universe (KI) in order to experience the Game we call Life.

This "spiritual energy-matter" that composes all Life (as a Lifeforce with Awareness and Consciousness) goes by many names throughout history—but we find the idea first treated as <u>ZU</u> on cuneiform tablets of Mesopotamia.

On an Identity lifeline of ZU energy, all Alpha Spirits are operating from a Spiritual Universe. We refer to this as the ZU-line on the Standard Model.

ZU is the name given to the spiritual essence of all Life in existence—and Self is a concentrated center or focal point as a ZU-continuum or Identity.

The True Self of an Individual Human is a "spiritual universe cause" of "physical universe effects"—engaging as an immortal Alpha Spirit with a Self-determined Will actualized as an Awareness along the ZU-continuum, extending from Infinity-to-Infinity, through every possible frequency and vibration along the total spectrum of physical and metaphysical existence.

THE SYSTEMOLOGY PRACTICES OF SPIRITUAL ADVISEMENT & COUNSELING SERVICES FOR MARDUKITE ZUISM.

The Mardukite Chamberlains were established in 2009 dedicated to recovery and consolidation of all historical, scriptural & ritual records of ancient Babylon in Mesopotamia. In 2011, a Mardukite faction (International Systemology Society) began to research and develop methods to apply ancient wisdom as a futurist spiritual technology that awakens, unlocks and fully actualizes spiritual potential of the Human Condition.

A systematic approach to spirituality is seen on the Standard Model, where ZU-line frequencies are represented at various degrees: "zero-point" body death; cellular activity and sensory perceptions of a genetic body; bio-chemicals induced by emotion; thoughts and intention transmitted between our Alpha Spirit and the "genetic vehicle"—all the way "up" the scale to a perfected clarity of Self-Actualized Awareness of I-AM as our true "Alpha" state, just below Infinity and Absolute Beingness.Full potential of ZU in Consciousness is only altered from its natural state as a result of personal fragmentation of the Human Condition. This may be restored with spiritual practices.

The Pathway to Self-Honesty is a personal journey and spiritual adventure marked by progressive clearing of spiritual energy channels fragmented by the imprinting and programming accumulated from experiences in our environment—the "debris" that fragments the total actualized experience of Self in Awareness as the Alpha Spirit.

The first and most important step—Before an individual can actualize potentials of the Spirit as Self, they must fully realize: the I-AM Self and the Alpha Spirit are One.

This state of Knowingness is the primary intention of basic spiritual practices found in Mardukite Zuism.

"Systemology" books and advanced training courses are also available to Mardukite Ministers seeking to qualify as specialized clergy, priests, priestess, and systematic processing pilots.

CREED OF MARDUKITE ZUISM.
PRINCIPLES OF BELIEF.[*]

1.) We believe in an Absolute Beingness, which is Infinite—the ABZU—the All-as-One encompassing Source of All Being, Knowing and Awareness to all Alpha (Spiritual-AN) and Beta (Physical-KI) states of existence.

2.) We believe in a spiritual energy of all Life and Awareness—ZU—in the physical universe (beta) that is an effect of a spiritual (Alpha) cause; a Spirit that is cause. This Spirit—in its Alpha state—is the True Self "I-AM" Individual Identity that many have called the "soul."

3.) We believe that the Human Condition is a genetic vehicle used by a spiritual source (AN) to experience the Finite as physical existence (KI)—that we are Awareness (ZU) projected onto a genetic vehicle—and that while the vehicle/body may perish to physical entropy, the "Alpha Spirit" remains immortal and Self-directed to the extent of its own Actualized Awareness.

---

[*]   First drafted in 2019.

4.) We believe that the highest form of worship and spirituality is the actualization and advancement of our "Self" as Spirit in Self-Honesty—and that Self-Honesty is the I-AM Alpha state of Being and Knowing, which is realizable in this lifetime.

5.) We believe that the purpose of all existence is: to exist—and that the prime directive of all spiritual Life is: continued existence of spiritual Life and co-creation of habitable Reality. "Good" and "Moral" actions are evaluated to the extent of this end.

6A.) We believe that no Life exists in exclusion to all other Life—and that the conditions of a habitable Reality extending from Self include:
Home; Community; All Humanity; All Life on Earth; All Life in the Universe; All Spiritual Life; and the Infinite.

6B.) We believe in a continued evolution of Alpha Spirit awareness developed beyond one physical life, and that a Spirit experiences many.

7A.) We believe Mardukite Zuism and its applied systemology is a 21st Century AD synthesis of the 21st Century BC wisdom collected on cuneiform tablets and experienced in ancient Mesopotamia, esp. Babylon.

7B.) This cuneiform library included details concerning: beings called the Anunnaki; ordering of the Cosmos; creation of Humanity; and an entire legacy of systematized traditions.

8.) We believe in the continuation of, and proper communication of, the true legacy of Human history—and the ability of every Human to realize that they are a Free Spirit in a Free Zone of Self-Determinism: and no "evils" can affect intentions if an individual is spiritually Self-Actualized in Self-Honesty.

THE ARCANE KNOWLEDGE FROM
MARDUK'S TABLET OF DESTINY.*

1.) As above, so below;
On earth as it is in Heaven
an-bala ki-bala an-ba ki an-ba

2.) What the Mind believes, the Spirit reinforces
da-ga nam-ku-zu dingir-Lamma a bi-ib-gar

3.) When disaster is self-made,
no man can interfere
*nig-ku-lam-ma dingir-ra-na-ka su—
tu-tu nu-ub-zu*

4.) What is given in submission
is a catalyst for defiance
nig-gu-gar-ra nig-gaba-gar-ra

5.) Whoever partners with Truth, creates Life
nig-ge-na-ta a-ba in-da-di nam-ti i-u-tu

---

* From *"Tablets of Destiny (Revelation)"* by Joshua Free.

THE ANUNNAKI EPIC OF

CREATION

MARDUKITE LIBER-E

The Babylonian Epic of Creation...

Named for its opening lines:
"When in the heights..."

—1—
THE MYSTICAL AND MAGICAL
TRADITION OF BABYLON

*"In the Enuma Eliš... it is Marduk who is now
given given credit for creating not only the
inter-dimensional portals, but also the BAB.ILI
Gateway of the Gods on earth—control of
which was usurped in Babylon."*

The *Enuma Eliš* cuneiform tablets are academically named for its opening lines—in Babyloni-
an-Akkadian language, meaning: "When in the
heights..." This series of seven clay tablets is
best known among both scholars *and* esoteric
seekers as the *"Babylonian Epic of Creation"* or
"Seven Tablets of Creation." They are *Babylonian* or Mardukite—venerating the Anunnaki
god *Marduk*—and not *Sumerian* (pre-Babylonian or *Enlilite*) in origin, as they are so often
misrepresented. In essence, they constitute the
main "systemology" of religious magic and
mysticism in Mardukite Babylon.

In 1849, archaeologists discovered the first copy
of the *Enuma Eliš ("e-numa elish")* series of
cuneiform tablets during an expedition of the
Royal Library of King Ashurbanipal in "Ninev-

eh." The tablet series debuted in public academically as George Smith's *"Chaldean Genesis"* in 1876, receiving critical global attention from historians, mythographers and biblical scholars —and not simply due to their antiquity, but because of how significant the work is when deciphering the secret "methodology" of Babylonian civilization: both its inner *esoteric* mystery tradition and its outward *exoteric* demonstrations of religion among the masses.

Scholars also determined the *Enuma Eliš* resonate so highly with the Judeo-Christian (Hebrew) *Creation-Genesis* epic that it was most likely the ancient source behind such Semitic primordial lore—yet virtually every seeker of *Mesopotamian Mysteries* will eventually run across the *Enuma Eliš* and will discover an understanding that is far deeper than any of the usual interpretations and diluted "bedtime story" renditions. The epic places emphasis on creation of humans and their ordered reality in the cosmos as demonstrated from within a specifically "Mardukite" worldview.

A critical examination of the *Enuma Eliš* reveals multiple levels or facets of potential holistic understanding. The discourse carries a "political" feature, while at the same time relaying its "theological" perspective in a most significant context for Babylonian systematization—specifically elevating the power of Babylon's patron god Marduk over the Anunnaki pantheon of Mesopotamia.

Literal interpretation of cuneiform tablets provides few clues toward a definitive differentiation between "religion" and "magic" (as we often describe such terms today) among ancient Mesopotamians of Babylon. In fact, outwardly among the general population, a distinction may not even have existed. However, more recent underground contributions of the modern "Mardukite" interpretation draw semantic lines with greater clarity than demonstrated in research of our academic predecessors. In this instance: the *esoteric* "magical" knowledge and higher learning of the priests, priestesses, scribes and magicians in contrast to the more *exoteric* "religious" demonstrations and general public understanding.

"Mardukite" appropriation of semantics distinguishes the purely *"Babylonian"* ancient *"Mardukite"* paradigm from its earlier *"Sumerian"* or *"Enlilite"* roots. Historically, a cultural emphasis toward a "Mardukite" (Babylonian) paradigm from *Akkadians*, *Assyrians* and *Chaldeans*—overshadowing and replacing a loosely organized "Enlilite" tradition of former *Uruk*

Sumerian and *Ur* dynasties that tended to focus on material politics and geographical conquest rather than spiritual and intellectual pursuits, such as we see later in Babylon with the rise of the scribe-priests and literary cults of the Anunnaki god Nabu, heir-son of Marduk and herald of the "Mardukite" tradition.

Cuneiform tablets that make any reference to Marduk and Nabu are purely "Babylonian" or a direct influence thereof. The elevation of Marduk in the Anunnaki pantheon clearly distinguishes this—using the first systematization of mass consciousness to seal the "Mardukite" tradition of Babylon as "World Order."

Earlier "Sumerian" civilization resembled a more "tribal" approach to the Anunnaki pantheon, observing a patron deity specific to the location, city infrastructure, natural resources and geographical terrain. This loose organization solidified and systematized for the first time in Babylon, host of the first official "national religion," but systematized under the "Mardukite" paradigm—which is equally reflected in practices and beliefs cementing the "magical tradition" of Babylon.

Usurpation and transfer of Mesopotamian "power" to Babylon, control of the empire by

priest-magicians and dragon-kings, literary catalogues of authoritative spiritual and religious
systems defining humanity and its relationship
with the Anunnaki "Sky Gods"—was all shown
or proved to be executed and systematized by
"Divine Right" and in accordance with the established "World Order" decreed by the Anunnaki Supernal Trinity—*Anu*, *Enlil* and *Enki*—in
prehistoric times...

> ...it was the *Enuma Eliš* that made this all
> possible.

The *Enuma Eliš* empowered the "Law of Marduk"—such as the Code of Hammurabi—in the
community. Marduk's "Creation Epic" also con-
tributed an intellectual and spiritual foundation
to all Babylonian magical and religious ceremonies. As a preliminary "rite" of invocation,
specialized priests and priestesses performed
dramatic reenactments from the tablet text—
such as those for personal "*gate-rituals*," the
"*maqlu*" rituals, and the Mardukite Spring Equinox Aries Festival of "*Akiti*" or "*Akitu*"—the
Babylonian "New Year."

As a cornerstone of political, spiritual and magical development in Babylon, the *Enuma Eliš*
is inseparably paramount to all related esoteric
and academic ventures—including any true *un-*

derstanding (and possible "theoretical" *imple-mentation*) of the ancient "Mardukite" Mesopot-amian religious paradigms, spiritual world-views, magical or occult sciences, and the later evolution of the same into various *kabbalahs* and "Mystery Traditions" throughout the world. The *Enuma Eliš* demonstrates transfer of Anun-naki power and Mesopotamian world-order to a "Mardukite" Babylonian paradigm, marking a significant turning point in global consciousness at its apex—again, apparent in all resulting ma-gical and spiritual practices and traditions.

A new brand of "Mesopotamia" emerges syn-chronous with the *Age of Aries—Age of Marduk* —appropriated mathematically as c. 2100 B.C. by ancient scholars. Babylonians elevated Mar-duk in the pantheon to coincide with a shifting era, clearly marked by Celestial Time—what we call "astrological ages" today. On the Spring Equinox, celebrated as the Babylonian New Year, the sun rises in a position relative to one of twelve equal sized thirty-degree zones en-compassing our celestial view of the cosmos like a band, each specifically distinguishing an era named for a correlating "zodiac" constella-tion. But the actual observed size of each con-stellation is not equal—some are larger, extend-ing past their "zone."

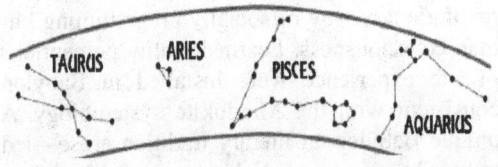

Conflict arose between a new "Mardukite" systemology and the former *Enlilite* standards due
to a discrepancy between the mathematical shift
and the visibly apparent or observed shift in Celestial Time.

The constellation of *Aries*—the *Ram of Marduk*
—is dwarfed by the sprawl of *Taurus*—the *Bull
of Enlil*—marking a preceding "Sumerian" age.
It seemed to "Mardukite" Babylonians that an
indigenous development period governed by
former *Enlilite* standards would never end! *For
when..?* asked Marduk.

Eventually a "Mardukite" Babylonian era did
arrive—but it was always contested and often
only allowed isolated points in history in which
to peacefully thrive. Since the new "Mardukite"
priest-scribes could not obviously wait for the
"stars to properly align," an elevation of Marduk in human consciousness would have to be
demonstrated another way.

The new "Mardukite" Babylonian era carried a revolutionary way of socially programming human consciousness. Learned reality perceptions of life experience were installed in Babylon consistent with the Mardukite systemology. A unique Babylonian literary tradition arose—led by scribe-priests of Nabu, son of Marduk—where societal use of a new refined form of cuneiform script made this possible. It was critical to a successfully ushering in a paradigm for the *Age of Marduk*; and perhaps the most profound demonstration of this was, in fact, the *Enuma Eliš* tablet cycle—for reasons that should become increasingly obvious to the Seeker.

In the *Enuma Eliš* text—the priest-magician is not only given the sacred keys to the "kingdom," but keys to *all* "kingdoms"—*on earth* as it is *in heaven*. The first six of the seven tablets are "tablets of ordering," which correspond to six primary "gates" or "veiled thresholds" fragmenting our existence from the *All* to manifest an energetically-condensed material reality. Significance of this correlation should be profound enough for seasoned *seekers* of these mysteries to make useful.

Many modern esoteric renderings treat the seventh tablet or "*secret tablet*" of the *Enuma Eliš* separately as an extension of earlier tablets. This is also reflected in our contemporary "Mardukite" literature, where the tablet series is cataloged as *Mardukite Tablet-F*, for the *Fifty Names of Marduk*, as a companion to *Mardukite Tablet-N*, the first six tablets of the *Enuma Eliš*.[*] Some go as far as to make the *Fifty Names of Marduk* the entire basis for a modern ritual "*spellbook*."

Following the inception of the modern "Mardukite" movement in 2008, a wide-spread revival of interest in the *Anunnaki*—and specifically the Babylonian god *Marduk*—has ensued: as planned, predicted and plotted during synchronized global ritual (intention-based) energetic movements or shifts in mass consciousness. These meditation exercises often coincide with what some call the "Beltane Gate" or "Fires of Bel" festival observed on "May's Eve" (April 30–May 1), roughly midway between Spring Equinox (*"Akiti"/ "Akitu"*) and Summer Solstice.

In contrast to the "magical" and "priestly" liter-

---

[*] Tablet catalog designations are indicated for "*The Complete Anunnaki Bible*," "*Anunnaki Bible (New Standard Zuist Edition)*" and "*Necronomicon: The Anunnaki Bible*."

ary tradition of Babylon, older *"Sumerian"* (or "Enlilite") texts emphasize documenting the many "firsts" offered by *Anunnaki* gods and developed as the "Arts of Civilization" toward establishment of the first cities in Mesopotamia. As time bore on, a new brand of "Babylonian esoterica" shaped systems of early human civilization, preserved within the knowledge base of priest-magicians, priestesses and scribes. This greatly furthered a class distinction not only between *Anunnaki* and humanity, but between select humans of an "elite" *esoteric* inner circle of understanding and those of the general population. This "magical" or "sacred" class of citizen—mainly kings, priest-scribes, and priestesses—served as intermediaries between what is *"divine"* and the more mundane worldly affairs of humanity.

Naturally the general population was only given (or capable of receiving) a diluted outward *exoteric* demonstration of higher mysteries of cosmic wisdom. These publicly visible "mythologies" are mostly all that has survived.

When compared to earlier pre-Babylonian *"Creation Tablets,"* one can easily determine the *Enuma Eliš* carries a much more advanced complex systematization with a wide array of intended applications.

The "outer teachings" were so influential (as the first "systemology") that they went on to affect not only Babylon, but also greater Mesopotamia and beyond—the Assyrians, Akkadians, Hittites, Phoenicians, Chaldeans, Semitic-Jews, and yes, even in Egypt, where *Marduk* was also known as "*Amon-Ra*" (and later "*Aten*" to priests of Akhenaton's secret Order). In contrast, purely "Sumerian" *Epics of Creation* are hardly "epic"—the whole cosmology often only briefly summarized in opening lines:—

> *AN carries off heaven;*
> *ENLIL carries off earth.*

After which *Enki* is given control of the first city—his home in *Eridu*. Eventually the "Arts of Civilization" are moved from *Eridu* to *Uruk* and Sumerian culture ensues, continuing to operate on this loosely defined simplistic methodology. It was rudimentary, but unchallenged, simply standing as its own as what *was* and *always had been* the case. This changed as "Mardukite" paradigms emerged with the inception of an "Ancient Mystery Tradition" permeating global spiritual and mystical factions thereafter —from *Kabbalahs* to *Hermetics*, and all throughout better recognized "arcane lore" and "esoteric sciences" imported by the Europeans in their own customs and traditions.

Marduk's spiritual and worldly supremacy is demonstrated on *Enuma Eliš* tablets as an epic describing his victorious conquest over the Great Cosmic Dragon of Chaos—TIAMAT. We can further appreciate the Babylonian opinions of Marduk when we couple to this lore of cosmic ordering the fact that Marduk also received a direct apprenticeship in the *esoteric sciences* and "Arts of Civilization" from *his father*, Enki, while residing in the ancient southern-most Mesopotamian city of *Eridu*—near the *Persian Gulf*—during much of the early "Sumerian" development period, where he is not ranked among the "Enlilite" Anunnaki pantheon and appears nowhere on pre-Babylonian tablet sources.

Prior to "*her*" identification on *Enuma Eliš* tablets as *Tiamat,* a Great Dragon of similar repute is found on older Enlilite tablets as KUR—also the *Sumerian* word for "mountain" that connects the "conquering of the dragon" with the "king of the mountain" motif—a concept explored elsewhere in our esoteric research library more thoroughly.*

---

* See "*Draconomicon*" by Joshua Free; also in the anthology "*Merlyn's Complete Book of Druidism*" by Joshua Free; and reissued in "*Merlyn's Complete Book of Pheryllt.*"

This ancient dragon-theme is so paramount—
eventually representing the god Marduk himself
—that it afterward appears in virtually all connected mythos defining "royalty," "divine right"
and "dragonblood." In fact, even earlier, we find
vague Sumerian attempts to show a similar
reign of power for the Anunnaki hierarchy, also
associating it with the "dragon"—or *Kur*. In
Sumerian epics, a "slayer of serpents" title is attributed to just about every figurehead among
Anunnaki *but* Marduk—and this would make
sense, if they are of a pre-Babylonian "Sumerian" origin. The fact that Marduk does not make
an appearance early on in the *Enuma Eliš* might
also suggest the epic is drawn from earlier
sources and/or meant to simply replace all previous (pre-Babylonian) Anunnaki mythographic
"claims" to authority. In all instances, this
"dragon-conquering" event is almost always de-
noting a "change in power"—a *paradigm shift*.

We can conclude that using a host of esoteric
knowledge from *Eridu*—and thereby *Enki*—the
priest-scribes of Nabu that developed the
Enuma Eliš (as national propaganda enforcing a
"Mardukite" church-state in Babylon) integrated
a legacy of secret wisdom and practical lore
from which the entire *corpus* of Babylonian magical curriculum is derived. It should also be

noted that as a "legal document" the *Enuma Eliš* transfers power to Marduk after first chronicling the alignment and control of the preexisting ruling cosmic order starting with:

> — the Primordial;
> — the Abyss;
> — the Dragon; then shifting focus to
> — the Anunnaki Supernal Trinity,
>   Anu, Enlil and Enki; and finally
> —Marduk as the hero of a
>   "younger pantheon."

The nature of the "A*byss*" and "*Primeval Dragon*" is treated more thoroughly elsewhere in our esoteric research library—particularly in "*Sumerian Religion*" (*Liber-50*)[*] and in "*The Tablets of Destiny*" (*Liber-One*).

Beyond the points already illustrated, *Enuma Eliš* tablets additionally allude to a dualistic fragmentation of existence. This dichotomy is demonstrated culturally in religio-political beliefs of "Babylonian versus proto-Sumerian," but also in terms of the interdimensional separation between the *heights* and the *depths*—the "seen" and "unseen" aspects of the All—and of considerable importance to a magician or mystic

---

[*] Also published as "*Anunnaki Gods: The Sumerian Religion*" (New Standard Zuist Edition).

seeking to understand the cosmos. These are treated as "AN" and "KI" in *Mardukite Zuism*, but semantics directly referenced in the *Epic* for this division graphically illustrates separation of the beast's two "halves"—the *dragon's head* and *dragon's tail* respectively:

> *Ti-a-mat e-Zi-ti* : "lower" Tiamat— "Body"
> *Ti-a-mat Shap-li-ti* : "upper" Tiamat— "Head"

Where many contemporary readers will be quick to recoil back to more familiar Semitic paradigms or Judeo-Christian frameworks—we can demonstrate connections there too. For example: in the *Book of Genesis*, the original waters (*"primordial abyss"*) were separated, giving rise to the "deep," rendered as *"tehom"* in Hebrew; but which is derived from Akkadian, *Tiamat.* What follows (in all accounts) describes an ordering of creation or systematization of the cosmos—the essence of materially condensed energies fragmented or separated from a "primeval source."

The ancient Babylonian magical tradition—or any magical tradition—is dependent on a practitioner's abilities to understand *true knowledge* of themselves, the cosmos, and the relationship between. Ever since the days of ancient Mesopotamia, these same magical traditions become increasingly dependent on the "local" (material realm) systematization of this knowledge as "magical correspondences." Although universal cosmic energies are a constant—as much today as in *Sumer*—any systematized division and classification of these forces appeared *first* in the Babylonian Mystery School, assigned in *writing* the *first* time for secret libraries of "Mardukite" priests, priestesses, scribes and kings.

Where many resources and materials over the past century and a half primarily deal with a base recovery of source texts and an interpretation of the outer *exoteric* mythographic understanding of cultures, the unique quality of the modern "Mardukite" literary contributions rests in its clear emphasis on the inner *esoteric* knowledge—not necessarily understood by the general populations of any era or region—maintained by those of the "*priestly*," "*mystic*," "*royal*" and "*scribal*" classes: those with established relationships with *Anunnaki gods*—and the cosmic forces they represent back of and behind the scenes of all religious, spiritual and political activity. This is the *real subject* of ancient Babylonian "magic."

— 2 —
A TRUE BABYLONIAN
"NECRONOMICON" GRIMOIRE

"Now that the fate of the Universe has been decreed. Now that the dyke and canal have been given proper direction; The banks of the Tigris and Euphrates have been established; O Anunnaki—Ye Great Gods: What else shall we do?—What else shall we create?"

As a staple of the Babylonian religious, political and magical tradition, we have demonstrated the primary historic significance of the *Enuma Eliš* in our previous chapter. Beyond academic, archaeological and even biblical studies, the first modern "New Age" incorporation of *Enuma Eliš* tablets for popular mainstream "Mesopotamian Neopaganism" occurs with the infamous "*Simon Necronomicon*" in 1977, where a bastardized rendition appears within it as the "*Magan Text.*"

Lore from *Simon's* book does loosely correlate with some magical elements of ancient Babylon, but it does not relate a complete tradition in itself, nor does it pretend to, styled after a "magician's notebook" and not truly an account of one that is initiated into a Babylonian priest-hood proper, or a specific Mystery School based thereupon—although the publication of the book has certainly gone on to directly incite formation of many quasi-orders and societies.

"*Simon's Necronomicon*" is not the main subject of *Liber-E*—(so as not to reiterate what appears in *Mardukite Liber-R**), but there are correlative aspects that often seem impossible not to mention when discussing modern "New Age" revivals Mesopotamian Neopaganism and the Mardukite Babylonian paradigm in the strictest esoteric or occult sense.

The fact remains that many people introduced to the Mardukite paradigm had already carried with them an affinity regarding mythology alluded to in "*Simon's Necronomicon*"; they were quite familiar with it, and hence the name has invariably stuck. Although we have now begun producing work without "*Necronomicon*" in the title—such as the present volume and even the reissue of our core source book as "*The Complete Anunnaki Bible.*" Ancient cuneiform tablets collected for the Mardukite system never

---

* "*Novem Portis: Necronomicon Revelations*" 10th Anniversary Collector's Edition and Deluxe Edition hardcovers by Joshua Free now available.

historically carried such a *title*, but this speaks only of its outer packaging.

The first six tablets of the *Enuma Eliš* epic—*Tablet-N Series*—clearly provide a scriptural basis for an ancient Mardukite Babylonian paradigm (and its modern revivals). We suspect its inclusion in all rites, rituals and meditations aligned to the specifically "Mardukite" interpretation of Mesopotamian mysticism, spiritual practice and personal systemology. Additionally, there is a seventh tablet of the *Enuma Eliš*, the *"Tablet of Fifty Names"*—*Tablet-F*—appearing more frequently than others in modern "Babylonian Magick" material; and, of course, it appears in *"Simon's Necronomicon"* and *"Spellbook"* sequel as a *"Grimoire of the Fifty Names of Marduk."*

"Simon's Necronomicon"—(also called the *Schlangekraft Recension* to those O.T.O. students of Kenneth Grant, or readers of his rather obscure "Typhonian Trilogies")—the *Magan Text* is introduced as a "lingering remainder" drawn from "sacred texts" of "cult priests" following the *"Old Faith"*—but, specifically described as a cult existing "at a time before Babylon was built..." Such statements may or may not have any true precedent on the *Enuma Eliš*; at the same time we know from the mere mention and

centralization of Marduk that the text cannot possibly be "pre-Babylonian"—clearly the "Seven Tablets of Creation" are *not* "Sumerian," but they *are* "Babylonian."

Original campaign efforts to install a "Mardukite" paradigm in Babylon actually began prior to a centralization of Babylon as a city or nation by cult-like Nabu-tribes in dedication to Marduk. These newly forming priest-scribes reinvented and refined civic, social and psychological use of cuneiform script—the "written word." A different style of script previously represented a more primitive and narrow application of writing the earlier *eme-gir* ("mother tongue") of the "Sumerians"—originally using fingernails to impress soft clay.

Greater widespread use of writing to represent human systematization resulted from invention of a reed-stylus "pen" by Nabu. The *stylus* allowed for a faster refined script, now used to create more influential writings, data collections, and records of history—all of which were meant to affect human consciousness. And this is how Babylonian tradition became the first systematized standard of ancient Mesopotamia.

But a pristine piece of paper folded once may just as soon be folded again—these methods of systematization unleashed on human consciousness were ever thereafter copy-and-pasted into all developing human cultures, then shaped and formed based on unique local geography, mythologies and language. This revised literary tradition supported developmental progression of early human society using themes we most conveniently identify as "magic" and "religion."

As with the Simon's "*Magan Text*," the historical *Enuma Eliš* tablets are a main *corpus* or body of instructional and supportive materials for the Babylonian ("Mardukite") priest-magicians, priestesses and scribes who aided ushering in a new metaphysical dynamic in human consciousness.

In addition to "setting the stage" for a ritual performance or ceremonial observance in the literal sense, the complete *Enuma Eliš* provides a mental "framework" ("paradigm" or "data-set") and an energetic link specifically to the "Marduk-current." The first six tablets "*empower*" the seventh, transferring authoritative power of the Anunnaki pantheon to Marduk; and combined they "*empower*" an effective spiritual hierarchy supporting complete practical realizations of Babylonian religious mysticism and magical tradition.

Contrary to popular "Hollywood" conceptions of ancient religion, magic and the *"Necronomicon,"* today the Mardukite tradition is revived in a greater state of Self-Honesty and dedication to cosmic wisdom. All of the literary materials suggest a focused dedicate intellectual and spiritual pursuit as a prerequisite of true initiation—which can only be bestowed from *"above,"* by authority and permission of the *"highest."* The power is not *in* the words, it is *in* the *Self*—the true and absolute *"I-Am"* that is really undergoing an initiation to paths representing cumulatively more advanced degrees of *awareness* and *ascension*.

Mispronouncing archaic words will not cause some primordial denizen to consume the operator; nor is any mere utterance of the *Enuma Eliš* sufficient to produce some "supernatural" result. The operator—*priest, priestess, magician, &tc.*—uses the tradition, system or standard as a "catalyst" to tap or activate very "natural" (but dormant) mystical connectivity with the cosmos, of which there are no "words" except those that truly and matter-of-factly resonant in consciousness exactly the nature of what they are meant to label. In short—the words and names can only carry the meanings given to them by an operator that pursued the true and underlying meanings.

The most ancient pure streams of mystical practice differ greatly from those more "Western" approaches popularly revived in modern "New Age" and metaphysical movements. Occult revivals tend to emphasize a focus only on elements that can be superimposed onto existing forms of modern magical practice or the esoteric obsession with obscure and popular "grimoires" that yield their best results in the form of self-delusion and thought-forms born from mental masturbation. Commonly, the seventh tablet of the *Enuma Eliš*—"*Fifty Names of Marduk*" (*Tablet-F*)—is revived in exclusion to the remaining lore, isolated as a modern "spellbook" or *short-cut* variety to tapping the total power of the greater "Mardukite" Mesopotamian legacy.

Several modern occult "writers" have demonstrated that the "*Grimoire of Fifty Names*" may be successfully employed by operators for strictly ceremonial magic forms of "spellcraft"—much like more famously used derivatives of the same: the *Goetia* or *Keys of Solomon*, which for all intents and purposes are rooted in a "Judeo-Christian" paradigm, and are not authentic "pagan" texts. Any real universal power exercised from the *Fifty Names* is activated by the preceding six tablets, demonstrating an older and more "priestly" methodology than what is traditionally prescribed in modern occult reconstructions. As a spiritual prerequisite, the six preceding tablets directly correlate to the first *six gates* that bring the *seeker* to the footsteps of Marduk for initiation and the opportunity to observe him as "Patron of Babylon" and King of the Anunnaki gods.

Since the modern inception of Mardukite tradition, a main tenet of the paradigm is repeatedly professed—the spiritual and magical abilities are not ends in themselves, but rather results from a true and faithful "Self-Honest" relationship with Anunnaki beings and the cosmic wisdom they definitely *guard*. After the first six tablets of the *Enuma Eliš* are intoned—after the operator passes through the first six "*gates*" (or *steps* on the "ladder of lights" or "stairway to heaven") and have attuned to the *gate-current* of Marduk, then and only then, may names and powers of the "seventh tablet" or any other *gate-work* from the BAB-ILI tablet texts given later in this current Mardukite "grimoire" anthology. This critical component is necessary to operate any of true Babylonian (*Mardukite*) *gatework* ("spiritual pathworking") or star-magic proper. By the seventh tablet of the *Enuma Eliš*, the priest-magician has assumed control of the "Mardukite" Anunnaki hierarchy and is conducting ritual incantations as if from the perspective of *Nabu*, acting on behalf of his father:

> *"The incantation of Marduk is the*
> *Incantation of Eridu;*
> *It is not I, but Marduk that speaks the*
> *incantation..."*

Invoking the "*Incantation of Marduk*"—or "*Incantation of Eridu*," as it is also called, is among the most prominent and widely revived aspects of the ancient Babylonian (*Mardukite*) tradition. But be aware that doing so strengthens a spiritual connectivity between the practitioner and this specific ancient, raw, and powerful alignment to the *Anunnaki*. Magic of this tradition is a "*holy magic*," originally reserved to a select group that maintained "higher" understandings of the universe and mythic symbols used to represent this knowledge. It definitively invokes powers of the Anunnaki by "birthright," calling on the ancient "covenant" alleged to be "sworn between the gods and man."

Authentic ancient concepts defined by the ancient "Mardukite" ideal in Babylon are revived in spirit today as work produced for *Mardukite Zuism* by *Mardukite Chamberlains*—a group of specific individuals seeking to free humanity from the spiritual and intellectual slavery that keeps us from the *Truth of Self*, and as a result has kept many individuals from a true *Self-Honest* spiritual evolution in this lifetime. Yes, we are "chamberlains" and stewards of an ancient mystery tradition; we serve the cause "on commitment" in dedication to the "*Highest*"—and not as some arbitrarily observed idol-worship in the name of *Marduk*, which is a commonly made mistake by outsiders and purely academic archaeologists.

Unlike traditional occult revivals—usually dependent on the *Kabbalah*, medieval *grimoires*, European peasant-folk traditions and other similar sources—the specifically *Mardukite* interpretation of what some brand "Mesopotamian Neopaganism" is actually rooted in an ancient pre-Christian, pre-Judaic paradigm from the "cradle of systematized civilization." We've coupled its writings with an exquisite balance of "New Thought" Systemology vocabulary that is most resonant with present times.

Although the greater legacy holds a wide-angle view of developmental progression of global systems *after* Babylon throughout the "Master Grades" of the Marduktie Academy, a modern *Mardukite* works *forward* in their understanding, starting logically at the beginning and following the course of systematic events and traditions as they have unfolded up until now—and possibly an insight into what is to come later. There is an authentic type of "high magic" employed in this tradition, but our best methodology is a "path" of practical processes promoting intellectual *Self-realization* and spiritual initiation, such as is reflected in our Systemology, used not only for advanced Mardukite work, but also by Mardukite Ministers for the Church of Mardukite Zuism.

Outward demonstrations of magical and mystic arts—such as "dramatic reenactments" or "ritual magic"—are only conducted from a point of *Self-Honesty* and not *self-delusion*, which is another common flaw in many of the more widely spread modern "occult" traditions. A powerful Self-Honest magician, priest or priestess is not waiting to become the *effect* of their own *cause...*

> *The gods help those who help themselves;*
> *they tend to make the able 'more' able.*

As relayed in *Mardukite Zuism* and *Systemology* knowledge lectures: All power comes from *Self*, the true "alpha spirit" or "I-AM" within-and-as *Self*. Any system, teaching or method that displaces focus of power and connectivity to the *All-as-One* "Source" away from *Self* is a deception.

If we are to classify the practice as "magic," then such a word is defined proper as: *Self*-directing the *Will* of the true *Self*. These terms should not be used to glorify the "artificial ego-self" developed in *this* world—an artificial facade personality worn by the *Self* as a temporarily sheath of true identity. To be successful, it is this mortally fabricated persona that practitioners of mystical arts must shed from their mind like snake-skin.

Modern practices of similar repute—often dubbed "ceremonial magic"—typically adhere to strict ritual criteria. When not arbitrarily added to a ritual for ridiculous purposes, many traditional magical, spiritual and/or religious practices are performed in *imitation* of authentic events first observed and recorded at the most ancient temple-shrines. Obviously this legacy went on to affect not only local populations, but later-derived practice of "Hermetic" traditions of ancient magick on a global scale—and often attributed to the original "Cult of Nabu" but recognized by the relative local language-name defining "Mercurian scribe-librarian gods"—whether *Nabu, Nisaba, Thoth, Hermes, Mercu-*

ry, Apollo, Tir, Ogmha, Menrva, Seshat, Teshmet, A'As, Odin, Tiwaz, Tyr, Anahita, Minerva, Mergen or *Merlyn...*

Modern *Mardukites* describe three aspects (or types) of magic or ritual found within the *Mardukite* work inspired by ancient Babylon:—

FIRSTLY...the work that leads to *Self-Honest* knowledge and experience of *Self* and the *Anunnaki*—a true and faithful dedication is prerequisite to all Mardukite Babylonian practices in general. One might classify this first form of "magic" as "prayer"—based on transmission of intention, establishing a relationship, and a clear communication channel with "spiritual" forces that one is later acting as an intermediary ambassador or "priestly" catalyst. Systematic prayer-books—of clay tablets, of course—were kept in private collections and bed-chambers of many successful ancient kings, priests, princesses and priestesses in Babylonian history.

This part of the *Pathway* is primarily "introspective" and "personal" in nature—meant to properly prepare an individual for ascent up the "stairway of godly evolution." It may also be studied, researched and developed among couples, groups, large orders and even priesthoods, just as it once was quite definitively in ancient times—and perhaps even among an un-broken underground stream since then.

SECONDLY...the *Anunnaki Star-Gate System*—which Babylon is boldly named for directly. As with most "*true magic,*" this type of exploratory practice is also "introspective" and to such an extent that it consists of only the most secret "*private esoteric*" practices of the Ancient Mystery School ("priesthood," &tc.), sharing in a relationship with the *Anunnaki* that is not as evident in the more *public exoteric* demonstrations, folk-beliefs or customs within the range of common knowledge. It is the ways of the uninitiated folk—and traditions prepared for their benefit—that most dry academic and archaeological interpretations are derived.

As a method of practice and tradition of personal development, the Gate motif of Babylon—also known to some as the "*ladder of lights*"—is not concerned with further accumulation of additional fragmented energies or "layers of consciousness," but rather the removal of these "artificial light filters" that inhibit *Self-Honest* experience of the "mystical" unity of *All-as-One*.

Secret tablets reveal that these fragmented "levels" and "layers" are representations that the

Anunnaki influenced as systematic parameters of awareness—what humans were capable of experiencing of reality.

This *cosmic* oriented practice could be classified as a "Celestial" form of Ceremonial Magic. But, this is not necessarily the same, one-to-one, with the contemporary understanding of what is called "Ceremonial Magick" today. In fact, this gauge of work is only treated in Mardukite "Grades" of Systemology. And yet, at the same time, archetypal Mesopotamian practices of "high magic" did later evolve into more familiar popularized systems of Greco-Egyptian "Hermeticism," European Druidry, and the traditional forms of Hebrew Mysticism, better known as the "*Kabbalah*," which directly evolved from Babylonian Star-Gate lore, as did much of the the entire "Babylonian Talmudic" and Rabbinical tradition established afterward by the Jews.

THIRDLY...the *Cultural Magic* most closely identifiable with what anthropologists and archaeologists are likely to study—quite frankly because it is the only aspect of ancient tradition that allowed for public observation and participation.

Compared to previously described "religious" and "celestial" forms, this practice qualifies the

84

title of "low magic" in many respects. It reflects everything we come to expect from a cultural archetype (and stereotype) of *Babylon* proper—the national rites of public spirituality and religion that further strengthened the "system" and the popular belief in it among the population. There is no shortage of archaeological evidence to support an *outer tradition* rich in colorful thematic annual festivals; ritual gestures, idol-statues, talismanic amulets and wards to accomplish protective, fertility and healing effects; even the personification of negativity, pestilence, demons and wicked-doers (*witches* and *warlocks*) are symbolically destroyed and burned in effigy as described on the *Maqlu* tablet series.*

An elementary description of ceremonial instruction may be derived from the *Mardukite Tablet-Q* series:

> "...make an invocation prayer to *Marduk* and *Sarpanit* and then invoke the Supernal Trinity—*Anu, Enlil* and *Enki*—followed by a conjuration of the fire and

---

* See *"The Maqlu Ritual Book"* edited by Joshua Free; *Tablet-M* series as found in *"The Complete Anunnaki Bible,"* and in *"Anunnaki Rites: The Maqlu Ritual Book"* New Standard Zuist Edition.

four beacon-lamps of the four watch-towers. Then perform the *Incantation of Eridu* and call forth a presence of your personal watcher *'sedu'* guardian-spirit."

Some basic modern applications may be respectively adapted from the following materials as they appear within this book and supporting Mardukite Esoteric Research Library and Anunnaki Legacy literary collection:—

- The "Incantation of Eridu." *Liber-W* or *Tablet-Y.*
- Conjuration-incantations of the Four Watchtowers: the four corners of the cosmos (and their *gate-seals*). *Complete Book of Marduk* (new *Liber-W*) or *Tablet-X.*
- Conjuration-incantations for the fire: the god-fire, fire-god, beacon-lamps, cauldron, candles, &tc. *Maqlu Ritual Book* (*Liber-M*) and *Tablet-Y.*
- Invocation-prayers to the Anunnaki "Gates of Babylon," the Supernal Trinity and Babylonian Pantheon (including representative *gate-seals*). *Liber-W, Tablet-B* and/or *Liber-50.*

In Simon's *Necronomicon Spellbook,* a practical use of the *Fifty Names of Marduk* is suggested, quite reminiscent of modern spellcraft more than any other ancient practice—and most importantly: skipping the essentials for traditional ritual magic, of Babylon or otherwise. And while some traces of our methods appear in the original Simon volume, the later released frugal *spellbook* emphasizes only information of the seventh *Enuma Eliš* tablet (sometimes indicated "Tablet-VIb" by scholars) concerning the *Fifty Names* of Anunnaki power usurped as "Names of Marduk" (*Tablet-F*) for *hierarchical magic* in Babylon. The Mardukite Esoteric Research Library offers a more complete and *Self-Honest* relay of this specific Babylonian (Mardukite) paradigm of ancient Mesopotamia than ever before.

The language for Babylonian Anunnaki "incantation-prayers" and "gate invocations" are essentially synonymous with each other, differentiated only by intention or applying a few statement lines. Those appearing in the Mardukite *Liber-W* (or *Tablet-W*) series—known as *The Book of Marduk by Nabu*—denote a very strong and deeply powerful devotional system adopted by priest-magicians, priestesses, scribes and dragon-kings of the ancient Babylonian Empire. The religio-spiritual practice is indicates a harmonic relationship with the Anunnaki "*gods*."

Petitions and prayers made before images of the gods in temples or private shrines may have yielded "spell-like" results, but as a "holy magic" that is not typically observed in contemporary "New Age" system-traditions. The powers of *above* are not "pulled down" by force and coercion, or by cryptology of some secret number and name, but are based on natural laws of *attraction*, *equity* and *vibration*, earned as "graces" by living the "Right Way"—a pious life dedicated to all that positively promotes *Life* in harmony with Cosmic Law.

— 3 —
MAGIC OF BABYLONIAN STAR-GATES

*"My spell is the spell of Enki. My incantation is
the incantation of Marduk. Power and blood of
Marduk is within me. It is not I, but Marduk,
who performs the incantation."*

The purpose of this *Liber-E* supplement—and
the *Liber-51* text it appends—is to provide sufficient foundations of historically accurate teachings of *esoteric lore* and *cosmic law* from the
Ancient Mystery School, in order to base a
modern tradition. From this we expect modern
practitioners, or esoteric archaeologists at the
very least, to glean a new interpretation of ancient Babylon and its spiritual, magical and otherwise national religious tradition. For some,
the literary legacy we provide is a god-sent to
incite an evolution of revivals and reconstructions found amidst the *"New Age"* today—and
its progressive development as *Mardukite
Zuism* and *Mardukite Systemology*.

A magician, priest or priestess operating at any
period in history may in fact benefit from Babylonian cuneiform "incantation" tablets so long
as they are employed within the appropriate

Mardukite paradigm. Tablets describing the *Anunnaki gods,* and the *Stargates* of Babylon they represent, are primarily given as "incantations." Unlike traditional catalogues of knowledge we might create today, Babylonian systematization is very carefully hidden within a body of tablets describing a handful of epics— but the "incantations" appear more abundantly than anything else. It is from these religious and magical tablets that we draw details about the individual figures, rendering additional insights that, for example, reading the *Enuma Eliš* tablets in isolation would not provide.

Over the past century, the most frequently cited Babylonian incantation tablets mainly pertain to the "*Lifting of the Hands*" series, made popular through academic translations unleashed from the British Museum since the early 1900's. The series is named for a common ceremonial gesture used in "praise" or "adoration" of the *sky-gods* or *Highest.* The standard gesture of priests and priestesses is displayed on some statue images of *Nabu* and *Teshmet* where the hands are resting in front of the body, with the right hand clasped around the left wrist.

Our modern premise for a magical mystical spiritual revival of Babylonian tradition begins with the idea that the *Enuma Eliš* is far from primitive—that these *Seven Tablets of Creation* are a basis for programmed material reality received by the most antiquated systematized societal civilization on the planet for our *current* cycle of history. Surpassing even this, for practical purposes of modern esoteric experimentation, there is a strong *sevenfold* structure present and observable in ancient Babylon—the same *sevenfold* theme defining an basis for relevant archetypal or common correspondences: numbers, planets, colors, notes of music, &tc. We can see evidence for a *sevenfold* fragmentation of the *All* everywhere we turn in this condensate Physical Universe.

> The very *sevenfold* lore that gifted Babylon its name—*Gates of the Star-Gods*—led to a greater codified systematic understanding of the world; and eventually *all* worlds. Esoteric practitioners and commoners alike still operate under its *spell* in present time.

When we consider our division of the visual spectrum of color; the audible range qualifying notes of music; the methodology behind the seven original sacred cities in Mesopotamia—considered energy points or even space ports by some scholars; the ordering of the "rays," "levels" or "days" of creation/manifestation;

and, above all, a representative ritual or ceremonial observation of the whole thing—physically displayed by *seven-stepped ziggurat* "high temples" of Babylonia... a spiritual, philosophical and religious standard becomes clear—one that is easily adapted for basic modern-day exploration and experimentation.

As a hermetically sealed system in Babylon, the standards put forth by the *Enuma Eliš* demonstrate a clear spirto-magical and religio-political sentiment motivating the account—specifically as it relates to elevation and centralization of *Marduk* within a greater Mesopotamian Annnnaki framework. By entrusting *Marduk* with a position as *King of the Gods*, he became responsible for the "ordering" of the physical universe—or cosmos as perceived by evolving humanity—a race first bred as a superior work animal, then upgraded yet again by *Enki* for the modern design humans are evolving from today. But we also know that beneath this programming lies the very cosmic code of the ancestral *god-race*, and that the proper use of the *esoterica* they have left behind for us is, in turn, a "map" that may guide the "unfoldment" of dormant spiritual evolutionary potential.

First established on earth by *Enki* in *Eridu* (proto-Sumerian), and then "transferred" by *Inanna-*

Ishtar to her city of *Uruk* (Uruk-Sumerian), the *Enuma Eliš* demonstrates an additional transfer of Anunnaki power and world order to Babylon during the "Age of Aries" shift—with it, control of the *Arts of Civilization* and the keystone called the *Tablets of Destiny*.

"*Tablets of Destiny*" are alluded to throughout Mesopotamian lore. And yet without concrete academic information to explore, the concept of such a relic was pushed into the realm of legend —to the same proportions as other "mythic books" of renown. More recent Mardukite Systemology discoveries regarding this ancient lore are found in the volume "*Tablets of Destiny (Revelation)*" (*Liber-One*) released in 2019.

In regards to the *Enuma Eliš*—the *Tablet of Destiny* is first in possession of the great primordial dragon *Tiamat*. She attaches it to *Kingu*, her vizier-messenger or quality of action and communication across the Abyss. After *Marduk* defeats *Kingu*, he removes the *Tablet*; attaching it to his breast, he assumes the same empowerment of authority and power—and it is this unique talisman contributing to his victory over *Tiamat*.

Considering all collected lore of the *Tablet of Destiny*, *Tablets of Destiny* or *Tablet of Destin-*

ies, the work—if literal—would be synonymous with collected *cosmic wisdom* or *secret knowledge* of the "gods."* Traditions that inherited Babylonian systemology (in part) later understood the same as a *Book of Life*, or among mystics as the *Akashic Records*, *Arcane Scrolls* or even *Arcane Tablets*—a hidden core of secret doctrine behind the Ancient Mystery School.

BABYLONIAN SEVENFOLD PANTHEON

Mesopotamian	*Sabian*	*Classical*
SHAMMASH	Samas	Sol, the Sun
NANNA-SIN	Nanna-Sin	Luna, the Moon
NERGAL	Nergal	Mars, Ares, Zivis
NABU	Nebo	Mercury, Woden
MARDUK	Bel	Jupiter, Thor
INANNA-ISHTAR	Beltis	Venus, Freia
NINURTA-NINIB	Kronos	Saturnus

~ Robert Graves, *"The White Goddess"*

If we are to take them as a metaphysical construct, then we can assume—as E.A. Budge ori-

---

* Also called the "ME" as described in *"Tablets of Destiny (Revelation)"* by Joshua Free.

ginally translates—that these are *Tablets of Fate*, though we know ancient Mesopotamian languages viewed "fate" and "destiny" as two different aspects, unlike today where semantics are often blurred. In short—as described in Reed Penn's foreword to "*The Tablets of Destiny*"—a "*destiny*" is a irrevocable inevitable "*destination*"; where "*fate*" is a pathway chosen to reach that "*destination*."

When the *seeker* combines a traditional seven-fold-schema knowledge base with corresponding *Anunnaki* figures represented by planets and days of the week, it is easy to see how a complex system developed. Both physically (the seen, the below, the earth) and metaphysically (the unseen, the above, the cosmos), each of the seven aspects are described as a particular "quality" or "nature" of the *totality* of existence —or else the *All* fragmented into "*sever*-al" parts more easily beheld or classified than the pure mystical unity that has no names or numbers and is known only to the *Highest* cosmic order—and true "initiates" of the *Highest*.

An *All-as-One* continuity may be fragmented by consciousness into any number of "fractions," each making perfect sense, fit within a context of total wholeness of "parts." In Babylonian tradition, this is observed as *seven*, and we can assign or reduce all aspects from other schemas back to this if we choose—dividing colors, lights, sounds and aspects into a two-fold (duality), three-fold (triads) and elemental four-fold paradigms in most popularly known occult traditions, yet they may also be assigned to a seven-fold division of reality described on Babylonian tablets. We can also see how the Babylonian Star-Gate system expanded or evolved into the traditional ten-fold *kabbalistic* models, demonstrating seven gates of the "younger" Anunnaki pantheon with the "Supernal Trinity" added to the system—and seven plus three equals ten.

An entire lifetime—perhaps several—may be spent decrypting a myriad of appropriated names and lore from various "mythologies" spanning all times and places. However, it becomes clear that the "visible spectrum" of archetypal energies—as we receive, perceive or experience them—is best documented and relayed in original source texts of the Ancient Mystery Tradition from Mesopotamia—and in many cases, specifically Babylon.

Each key "quality" of existence—or *ray* of the spectrum—is directly associated with key figures of the Anunnaki "*pantheon,*" a systemology or model of understanding all aspects of the cosmos—it is not restricted only to Meso-potamian or Anunnaki applications. As a result, we find so many direct correlations to later emerging "mythologies" that it would detract from the current purposes of this volume to discuss further. It is enough to draw attention to this point.

In the oldest tradition of Babylon, with literary origins significantly predating classical mytho-logies, we are given, for example, the role in a pantheon represented by the planet *Jupiter*—re-cognized as the position of *Enlil* in older Sumerian lore, but identified with *Marduk* for actual systematization of Mesopotamian esoter-ica. This position shares particular "religious" affinity for services held on Thursday, which we name for *Thor*—the Norse "*Jupiter*" &tc.

Retained within the "ancestral spiritual tradi-tion" of Mesopotamia, the "elder pantheon" is observed as a "Supernal Trinity" extending out-side "visible" or traditionally accessible aspects of creation. This means ancient Mesopotamian astronomers may have had some "otherworldly" knowledge of more than the "ancient seven vis-ible planets," but their astronomy logically in-cluded only those that were "visible" to the na-ked eye—those carrying the greatest observable influence felt here on earth. We find the representatives of a "Supernal Trinity" beyond (or "above") the *seven* and also encompassing them —and we see its influence in the traditional "*kabbalah*" ("*cabala*" or "*qabala*").

Suffice it to say that where ancestral figures—or Elder Gods of Sumer—such as *Anu*, *Enlil*, and *Enki* appear frequently in older sagas, it is the offspring of these gods—the "younger pantheon" of Babylon—that represents the more visible and accessible forces of the universe. These are the forces that constitute the main substance of spiritual, mystical, magical and religious work. Above, beyond and more widely encompassing the "ten-as-one," we find three additional spheres—called "*ains*" in the Semitic Kabbalah—the ALL, the Abyss and the Dragon. When we approach the mysteries of ancient Babylonian Tradition and read from tablets like the *Enuma Eliš*, we actually glean an even greater esoteric understanding of these mysteries than thought academically possible.

Magical power, spiritual evolution and mystical arts all represent a deep understandings of the energetic relationships between all forces in the cosmos—and in truth, all aspects in the universe are connected as a continuity—but it is the key correspondences from "our side" of reality that form base knowledge contributing to many pop-

98

ular modes of "New Age" thought, tradition and
occult practice. It is difficult for many to to understand the simplicity of the original and most

---

TRADITIONAL SEVENFOLD
FRAGMENTATION

I. Sunday: Sun—Light
II. Monday: Moon—Division (of Waters)
III. Tuesday: Mars—Dryness (land, pasture)
IV. Wed: Mercury—Celestial Bodies (stars, cosmic order)
V. Thur: Jupiter—Primordial Life (plant, sea-beast, bird)
VI. Friday: Venus—Terrestrial Life (land-beasts, humans)
VII. Saturday: Saturn—Repose

~ Robert Graves, "The White Goddess"

I. —Light
II. —Particles
III. —Atoms
IV. —Molecular Matter
V. —Plant Kingdom
VI. —Animal Kingdom
VII. —Completion

~ Douglas Monroe, "Deepteachings of Merlyn"

ancient traditions because of how much has been obscured, added and encrypted. Until we shed this skin—overcoming a lifetime (or more) of personality-programming—we will always be restricted to see *the totality of reality specific only to our own set of "lenses."*

The fundamental sevenfold Anunnaki "gate" system of Babylon presented within this "grim-oire" clearly has many "*esoteric*" applications—of which its foremost (and original) purpose being: the "sealing" of reality, meaning the perceptions of energetic experience throughout the cosmos, or else (at its most rudimentary level), what humans consider "truth" in regards to "existence."

> This includes what we know (*and not-know*)
> of our origins (*in the past*) and the
> purposeful utilization of
> knowledge (*in the present*)
> toward an appropriately destined future.

But it is this "future" aspect that always remains in debate. There is no consensus as to the "best use" of active energies in the present.

The spiritual evolution of the human species—its spiritual "*hybridization*"—is entirely dependent on an intentional "return" to the *Source of All*.

Just because there is no "common vision" among the masses, does not mean that the *seeker* commits error in following this path. Quite the contrary.

It has always been the case that a select few—the highest minds and magicians among society—are those responsible and in power to affect and shape the general global consciousness.

It is these folks, who have themselves walked the "ladder of lights" or "stairway to the stars" and returned among men.

— 4 —
CLIMBING THE STAIRWAY TO HEAVEN

"The length of the animistic period of religion in Babylonia is not known, but there is abundant evidence that by the fourth millennium B.C., the Sumerians had formulated a system of gods in which each held a well-defined place."

—E.A. Wallis Budge, *"Babylonian Life & History"*

Relaying the inter-dimensional model of *"Star-gates"* would be much easier if we could do it in a *linear* fashion—the way we understand and learn most things in a very condensed physical material world. But such is not the case—rendering most 2-Dimensional depictions of any real *kabbalistic* system very "deceptive"—models that tend to emphasize the division of "levels" and *"fragmentation."* But *"Veils of Existence"* are just that—*veils*. They may enshroud what we experience of existence, but they can not truly divide or separate the *All* from the *All*. They can only further fragment what they are created from with more *veils* and more perceived levels of semantic division—of which esoteric sects and occult orders have found little difficulty in doing throughout time.

Babylon is best named for its paradigm—a "stairway to the stars"—an iconic representation of the seven-leveled *high temples* of Marduk and Nabu. These *ziggurat* pyramids demonstrated the "visible" spectrum of energy radiating between the "heavens above" and the "earth below"—meaning all of existence between the unknowable "heights" and "depths" of the cosmos. *Bab-Ili* texts cited throughout modern Mardukite literary work and esoteric (spiritual/mystical) experimentation are collected references from throughout greater cuneiform tablet collections. This original name for its system, nation, city and peoples—*Bab-Ili*—is the word for "gate," "doorway" or "entrance" combined with "god," "star," or "heaven."

Although ceremonial (ritual) methodology of *"gatewalking,"* *"gatekeeping"* or *"starwalking"* is traditionally traversed from an Earth-oriented sequence (e.g. the *first gate*, or Earth zero-gate), instruction of a Babylonian "systemology" for esoteric magic, spirituality and religious mysticism is best aligned to the *Enuma Eliš*—from the beginning...

In the beginning...the *Ancient of Days*—before time and space had been fragmented into existence; before the heaven and earth had come into existence; before reality was separated into existence—there was simply the *All-as-One*—the *Absolute*; all existences as *One Existence*; all being as *One Beingness*...

WHOLENESS FRAGMENTATION

ALL-as-ONE

\ /

The Primordial Abyss

\ /

The Primeval Dragon

A full detailed sequence of fragmentation is explored within "*Sumerian Religion*" (*Liber-50*). We can summarize key points here as they apply to theory and practice of magical and mystical traditions of a Babylonian Anunnaki Pantheon.

Regarding "*Wholeness Fragmentation*"—or the ALL—we refer to an Arcane Tablet of Ancient Systemology that states:—

"Other than *The Law*, there is but *Infinity*, which is *Nothingness*. But in that *Infinity of Nothingness*, there is *Unmanifest*, the *Latency, Possibility, Futurity, Potentiality*, and promise of *Manifest Everythingness*. It is the *Chaos* from which, under *The Law*, emerges the Cosmos. It is the *Womb of the Cosmos*."

Therefore the ALL took on a beingness of its own, embedded into ALL entangled existence as a state of "*Infinite Manifestation*" ("*potentiality*")—subordinate to the *Primordial Abyss*.

When the *waters* were separated to give rise to the *First Form,* the *First* Cause—the *Primeval Dragon* separated as active consciousness and energy in motion.

This separation from the Source is *Ego*— the perspective or consciousness of the cosmos—knowledge and motion, represented by a "creature" which rose out of the "depths" of the "infinite sea" to give *form* and *function* to a "manifest universe."

It is from the start that many metaphysical schools of thought and occult lodges mistakenly confuse the terms of *Absolute Law* and *Infinite*

Nothingness. "*Absolute Law* is not an infinite capacity for expression of power—it is *Power-in-Itself.*"

SUPERNAL FRAGMENTATION

<u>ANU—The Heights (Uranus)</u>
\ /
<u>ENLIL—The Airs</u>
\ /
<u>ENKI—The Deep (Neptune)</u>

Celestial fragmentation—manifest reality in consciousness—appears in the Sumerian Anunnaki paradigm as the "Supernal Trinity" represented by the *Heavenly One* [ANU], the *Lord of Air-Space* [ENLIL] and the *Lord of the Deep Earth* [EA–ENKI]. These ancestral figures appear as "Elder Gods" in the Babylonian pantheon—or recent themes like the "*Necronomicon*" in the New Age. This progression is not progenerative—both *Enlil* and *Enki* are sons of *Anu*—but it does illustrate the hierarchical division or fragmentation of these *higher powers* concurrent with the highest three power stations or *kabbalah sephiroth.*

BABYLONIAN FRAGMENTATION
THE "BAB.ILI"

VII. NINIB/NINURTA—Saturn
∧
VI. MARDUK—Jupiter
/ \
V. NERGAL/ERRA—Mars
/ \
IV. SHAMMASH—The Sun
/ \
III. INANNA/ISHTAR—Venus
/ \
II. NABU—Mercury
/ \
I. NANNA/SIN—Moon
/ \

The BAB-ILI formation (sequence)—the *seven-fold path*—is based on a tradition specific to Mardukite Babylon, demonstrated in its correlation to the seven-fold stepped path to Ascension —a bridge connecting this condensed mundane physical world with the heights through a successive series of veils or fragmentation, shielding an individual from a Self-Honest experience. All of the "practical magic," or ritualized realizations of mystical energy used in Babylon, is reflected in this paradigm.

It is important that magical pursuits are always balanced with the mystic arts—for it is essential that the *seeker* does not fix too strongly to the plethora of "linear" representations of fragmentation that are possible (even within this specific paradigm).

The nature of the "fractured" universe beyond the *All-of-Existence* is "recursive" or "cyclical" if we treat it in a material sense. This idea is always represented by the universal symbol of the *Cosmic Serpent* encircling all of creation while devouring its own tail—the *Great Universal Dragon* unfolds its form to manifest all existence and beingness. And at its most concentrated level or degree—as is expressed in the *Enuma Eliš*—the head or consciousness of the dragon is indicative of "space" and the body as "matter."

It seems a mighty trick, but *infinity* as a material expression is only infinite by "recursion." The manifest Physical Universe cannot be truly "infinite" for such is a property, at best, of only the "potential."

RECURSIVE FRAGMENTATION

<u>ABYSS</u>
\ /
<u>HEAVEN</u>
\ /
<u>THE HEIGHTS</u>
\ /
<u>AIR-SPACE</u>
\ /
<u>THE DEEP</u>
\ /
<u>ABYSS</u>

Material or mathematical infinity is not always as we might imagine it. Although it carries a relative "endless" appearance, it is not necessarily "boundless" so much as it is "recursive"—repetitive and cyclic—which we have also demonstrated philosophically. In fact, it is a very symbolic but genuine representation of infinity that we use to designate an order or cohesion to the *seven* as All-as-One when we draw the figure "8" as itself, or on its side, to literally indicate an "infinity" sign. And by no esoteric coincidence, the "8" on a keyboard also coincides with the "*" asterisk, a symbol der-

ived in form and name from "*istari*," a cuneiform sign for "AN" meaning: "star" or
"heavens"—but most literally the word: "god";
and of which we treat in *Mardukite Zuism* as the
utmost Supreme Beingness.

Magic is not a "supernatural" art—on the contrary, it is quite "natural" although not a
"common" understanding among the masses.
Just as differing degrees of physical or emotional prowess are found in some, or intentionally
practiced and exercised by others, we find intellectual and spiritual gifts in a select few drawn
toward deeper *esoteric* understanding of themselves, the universe, and the connection
between. This is a very real energetic connection present throughout all existence and
between all peoples—some are naturally more
aware or actively sensitive to the constant interaction and energetic exchange taking place
throughout the cosmos, the Mind and the Body
at all times.

There is nothing "unnatural" about magic, except ironically the refusal of the population to
pursue this living awareness. This distinction
directly contributes to the obscure or secretive
aura radiated by individuals and groups that *do*
pursue these matters—because it is out of reach
and beyond the scope attained by a normative

"mundane" existence. The truth is that a person may very well get by an entire lifetime without taking notice of the bigger picture, and such a person will never understand why someone else would even bother with such "ridiculous trifles" or "dangerous devil-worship"—as they comprehend it.

Modern *seekers* will be quick to find numerous other applications for the BAB-ILI system—and will undoubtedly spend a great deal of time drawing parallels between this most ancient systemology and all of the traditions derived from the same lore. However, above all else, the true and original purpose of the BAB-ILI system is to develop a *Self-Honest* relationship with the *Anunnaki*, and in the process, a true and faithful *Self-Honest* awareness of-and-as *Self*. The *Self* is the real "I-AM" that is doing the "observing." All of the *filters* we assume in our lives, in our philosophy and our beliefs and assumptions about the world around us, are directly responsible for the interpretation of existence and reality for what is ultimately deemed true as "personal experience."

The *Babylonian Anunnaki Tradition* is the specific paradigm that takes precedence in ancient *Mardukite Babylon* and all magical lore connected to the BAB-ILI "gate system" of religious-styled spiritual work. The "gate-work" or "spiritual pathwork" is alluded to on clay cuneiform tablets as "prayers" and "hymns" to petition representative powers of the pantheon of *Seven* by name, and their consorts—"Divine Couples" often listed on the tablets as *Guardians of the Gates*.

As a true magician, priest or priestess approaches each of the *Gates* in true *Self-Honest* "devotion" and "dedication," this exploratory journey allows opportunities to develop a true understanding and practical access to the most raw, primordial and powerful currents of energy in the cosmos. This is reinforced by an *esoteric* use of what others will fail to see beyond an empty "religious lip-service" reflected in a daily regimen of meditation, prayer and ritual, coupled with a pious lifestyle and dedication to spiritual ascension. This is far from the methodology realized today among more common forms of organized "religion" and empty deity "worship"—particularly those paths that tend to promote a restrictive dependence on an organization or institution for all "routes to enlightenment" as opposed to *Self*, directly.

The very important Mardukite-specific semantic concept of *"Self-Honesty"* has been explored at great length throughout the *Mardukite Core* of literary materials—but more specifically its intellectual "New Thought" off-shoot branch, known as Systemology—but to clarify for present purposes:

> *Self-Honesty* is *not* simply "being honest with yourself"...

...as is generally assumed on the surface. It actually goes much deeper than this: *Self-Honesty* is the directed will of *Self* in a state of *honesty in Truth*—without a manifold array of the "many parts" and "fragmentation" serving as filters and programmed beliefs, many of which are unfounded, illogical or unnecessary and which contribute to what we have the ability to know and experience—or not.

The "*ladder of lights*" or "*stairway to heaven*" proposed in this paradigm is nothing short than the original methodology of systematic removal of these other filters that keep the *Human condition* from a *Self-Honest* experience and awareness of the *Cosmic Law* that is within-in-and-as all material existence—and which is the main subject of the upper-level Wizard's art. When we can see—historically and anthropologically—systematization of "civil humans" is structured within the ancient Mesopotamian paradigm, it should come by no surprise that the same "higher minds" responsible for this fragmentation would also have kept detailed records, even if only for their personal collections, of a "way back," the "key" to the "door" that leads *outside* of the system.

Some esoteric practitioners believe that the "*ladder-stairway*" is means for taking on *more* attributes, levels of false programming or layers of existence—as such, it is actually quite opposite. We already occupy an entangled spiritual existence in *sevenfold* fragmentation—something that Eastern traditions label as *chakras*, inter-dimensional energetic centers of the "body" connected to the *seven universal rays*. All "pathworking" conducted within this tradition is concerned with the energetic "refinement" of these filters, not accumulating or assimilating something *more*.

In every way, in all forms material, and in every aspect of energy that is defined by the *human condition*, the reoccurring theme within this work (and all true *mystical* work) is *Light*—and yet, this is not necessarily the same concept that is otherwise relayed in fanciful New Age lore or other "dualistic" moral doctrines. The *Light* is that which emerged from the void of the Abyss, the Infinite Nothingness. *Light* is the infinite made manifest and visible.

Where the All-as-One and singular expression of *Light* is an Absolute, we experience and encounter a fragmented spectrum—a unity divided to display rainbow arrays. True magic pertains to these same rays, but only as a means to access the singular and highest expression. The *Clear Light* and the *Seven Rays* are a part of us and everything that is around us, the very reason our experiences—whether "mystical" or "mundane"—*are* experienced as they are.

There are many recommendations throughout the "Mardukite Core" from which to compile a personal "grimoire." That being said, there are those who will at first be most interested in the ritual particulars, to which we provide the following list of suggested materials:

BASIC TOOLS OF MARDUKITE MAGIC IN BABYLONIAN ANUNNAKI TRADITION

- *Sigil-seals* of the Four Watchtowers.
- *Candles/Lamps* for the Four Quarters (Watchtowers).
- *Sigil-seals* of the *Anunnaki*: (Supernal Trinity and the Seven Younger Pantheon).
- *Gate-sigil* glyphs appropriate to a particular "level" or "step" on the "Ladder"; and/or "Gate" sign.

- *Cauldron* or *fire brazier* (consecrated).
- *Candles* or *lamps* to represent the "God and Goddess" (usually Marduk & Sarpanit in Mardukite-specific or Marduk & Ishtar in other versions), and likewise:
- *An image of your god and goddess* (altar statuary or visual/graphic art).
- *Seven Divine Decrees*, implements of the Divine Arts of Eridu in accordance with the ancient Sumerian Anunnaki Tradition.
- *Incense* or *herbal offerings* to be burned—frankincense, myrrh, sandalwood, pine resin, palm resin, &tc.
- *Water* and *salt* for ceremonial/ritual consecration.
- *Flour of Nisaba* or *Nabu* and *Teshmet*, to mark the boundary of the "magic circle" (consecrated).

Of the items previously listed, the one aspect appropriately deserving of additional comment —the *Seven Divine Decrees*. These symbolize legendary "articles" taken from Enki's possession at his city of Eridu by Inanna-Ishtar, which she brought back to her city, Uruk, subsequently moving the capital of early Sumerian development there.

In other mystic cuneiform-tablet sagas, these articles are described in Inanna-Ishtar's own cycle of "*Descent to the Underworld*"—but the purposes of a Babylonian magician or priestess, however, should be concerned with the "*Rising on the Planes*" in the opposite direction, using a *Ladder of Lights* described by the BAB-ILI system of Babylon to achieve true spiritual evolution to walk among the spheres as *gods*.

> Assuming ascension to "godhood" is always the *intention* of high magical arts, but seldom achieved through conventional "Western magick."

In conclusion, these "legendary articles" are most simply described as follows:

THE SEVEN INSTRUMENTS OF DIVINE DECREE

Shugurra — "*Starry Crown of Anu*" ("*diadem*")
Wand — of "*crystal*" (lapis lazuli)
Blue Necklace — of "*crystal*" (lapis lazuli)
Bag of Gemstones — presumably lapis lazuli
Ring of Power — usually "*golden*"
Frontlet Amulet — breastplate "*talisman*"
Pala — "*royal*"/"*priestly*" robes (garments)

THE EPIC OF CREATION

APPENDIX

OF LIBER-E

*A collection of esoteric supplements
released alongside Liber-E and
as an Appendix in former editions.*

EPILOGUE

"A Brave New Babylon Rising"
by David Zibert

Conflict. . . Unrest. . .
  On earth as it is in heaven. . .
At the precipice of a planetary evolution,
  the *world* ends.
    It always does. . .

Global tensions rise to unprecedented heights with the passing of each day. The *bright future* once wrought for mankind grows dark for the race as a whole. To it: arcane philosophy failed; ageless religion failed; humanistic ideals failed; and every magic spell and scientific formulae furthers sealing mortal man in his own self-made systematic prison, driving the coffin nail home—a single-track to travel upon furthering our journey into the *downward spiral* sending a world into inevitability. . .

                . . .apocalypse.

And this is my hope for the world, shared from the depth of my soul and joined in the voices of many self-honest truth seekers who have seen for themselves. . . renewal!

Mystics know; children know; even *birds* know— the world is *ending*. Of course, this does not imply blatant physical, material and totalitarian destruction of humans (so let us not employ the same scare tactics of every evangelizing preacher under the sun), it is instead the ending of *a human world*.

Recorded legends on ancient tablets point toward an era of *renewal* that will give way to the fabled *Golden Age*, a *Brave New World*—a true *new age*. But this is no *new* idea at all, rather it is something predicted by the main tenets of every true spiritual path throughout history, differentiated solely by semantics and appearing as varied as opinions from the *Second Coming of Christ* to the the cosmic collapse of the material universe by some rift in space-time or even *dark matter* and *black holes*.

You can label and interpret, even sugarcoat, what is happening any way you like—the simple fact remains: There is an undeniable feeling shared throughout the collective human consciousness that *something* is about to happen—that something *is* happening—and yet it all seems to endlessly cycle back and forth in some determined fragile balance... So *what* are we to do?

While the bungled confusion of the world plagues the mind with anxiety demons and victimization tendencies, the answer couldn't be simpler: *we must provoke the end of the world*, in this case, through a *massive paradigm shift*, meaning the necessary return of the *true spirituality*. By this, I mean the original *stuff*; untainted; undefiled through time by the analytical minds and personal truths of men corrupted into *systems*—fragmented from the whole; never the tween shall meet; *thank you, call back later*. It may seem like nothing new; but *no*, this time *it is different*.

In the wake of this self-honest planetary need for a *Great Awakening*, and on the cusp of a true *new age*, many "cults" have risen in recent past, loosely termed "pagan." Yet, in all of their once revolutionary efforts marked upon human consciousness, what they have to offer is often really only a "turn of the wheel," simply providing a different container for the *same content*, proving to us once again that humanity has not evolved much since the days of antiquity.

Understand we are not here to tell you what to think, raising our *"Mardukite literature"* to some new authoritarian heights, but we are offering critical information and data correction for your noggin so that you might *self-honestly* think for *yourself*. The emphasis here on *self* is not merely some glorification of individualism or newfangled ego-worship, but an affirmation that if we really want to change the *world*, we had better clean up and change our *self* first.

When each human being takes the responsibility to grasp the *self-honest* realizations of who they are and where they come from, what the world is and how it was made, of the stuff dreams and stars are made of, the *universe* and *everything*—when the experience of all these things can be done *honestly* from *self*, then the race will see an end to the current melancholy, heinous nonsense that is happening and has been happening for quite some time—a condition that is actually *anathema* to the survival of the very creatures that keep these things the way they are!

The premises we use to chart a *new world* are simple enough:

- *Every* human being has the potential and responsibility to experience life in *self-honesty*.

- *Every* human being has the right and freedom to demand this of their existence.

- *Every* human being has to embrace *some universal oneness* in order to live in harmony with itself as a race of brethren; with the Earth as a base of homestead; and with the universe as a matrix of existence. Only then can humans experience true *unity with all life, the universe and everything!*

This is our *true* and *destined* existence.

But what has kept man from achieving these ends? Why is it that the shortcomings of humanity throughout history seem to keep repeating recursively? Why has *everything* failed? As with all else, we find that the answer is again quite simple: *because humans are forgetful*. We forget easily; we are often sad; we suffer; we lose sight. To regain anything meaningful for the present and any hope for the future, we must remember what once was, and fortunately for us, an order of some of the earliest mystics thought of just that—so they created *cuneiform-writing*.

This book, as with the remaining "cycle" of literature produced by the *"Mardukites,"* is sure to present to you ideas of "history" and "magic" in ways you have never seen, or maybe even imagined before. The tradition that it represents does not deal in rudimentary hierarchical *grimoires* or the application of general hermetic principles upon some historical ethnocentric tradition. The "Mardukite" work runs much deeper than even this. It presents *The System*—the *archetypal* system—that has formed the basis for every mystery tradition to later emerge.

In other words: if you can correctly understand the means and motives of the mysteries and religion of Babylon and Sumer, you will correctly be able to interpret "history" and "magic" as a whole—whatever these words may mean to you. You will become privy to the beauty of the original efforts that have mostly deteriorated with time, probably attaining its lowest evolutionary depths in Christian-controlled medieval Europe – or even in the practices of modern day Jews and Muslims who use religion to shroud political reasons for killing one another. Even more important perhaps, you will become aware of what *really* happened in ancient Babylon, and understand whether or not it really was the *right* way to execute *Divine Order*, and why.

Indeed—the focal point of the modern *Mardukite* movement has never been about bringing back the *verbatim* "Babylonian paradigm" one-to-one, because this would only be the "turn of the wheel" again, and we've already grown dizzy and tired by such ventures. *This time*, it's all about fixing what went wrong, actually fixing the problem of *systems*, the root of all problems really, at the core. When every individual takes up the *Sword of Truth* against the world, executing the *acid test* of *self-honesty* on reality, then no doubt a *new*, better, *upgraded* aeon will really begin for mankind. This, we call: *New Babylon!*

To those who *also* feel called to pursue this with us, we say:

WELCOME HOME!

THE ENUMA ELIS

The Babylonian Cuneiform "Epic of Creation"
Mardukite Tablet-N Series and Tablet-F

TABLET I

When in the heights the Heavens had not been named; And the Earth had not yet been named; And the primeval APSU, who birthed them, And CHAOS, TIAMAT, The Ancient One, Mother to them all.

Their waters were as One and no field was formed, No marsh was to be seen; When of the gods none had been called into being, And none bore a name, and no destinies were ordained; Then were created the celestial gods in the midst of heaven, LAHMU and LAHAMU were called into being; And the Ages increased.

Then ANSAR and KISAR were created, And the god ANU then came forth who begat NUDIM-MUD [ENKI]. Abounding in all wisdom he had no rival. Thus the Great Gods were established. But TIAMAT and APSU were still in confusion, Troubled and in disorder. APSU was not diminished in might, and TIAMAT roared.

APSU, the begetter of the Great Gods, Cried unto MUMMU, his minister, And said: "MUMMU, thou minister that causes my spirit to rejoice,

Come with me to TIAMAT." So they went and consulted on a plan with regard to the gods, their sons.

APSU spoke: "Let me destroy their ways, let there be lamentation; And then let us lie down again in peace." When TIAMAT heard these words, she raged and cried aloud. She uttered a curse and unto APSU she asked: "What then shall we do?"

MUMMU answered giving counsel unto APSU, "Come, their way is strong, but you can destroy it; This day you shall have rest, by night shalt thou lie down in peace."

They banded themselves together; And at the side of TIAMAT they advanced; they were furious; They devised mischief without resting night and day. They prepared for battle, fuming and raging; They joined their forces and made weapons invincible; She spawned monster-serpents, sharp of tooth, and merciless of fang; With poison, instead of blood, she filled their bodies. Fierce monster-vipers she clothed with terror. With splendor she clothed them, she made them of lofty stature. Whoever beheld them, terror overcame him, Their bodies reared up and none could withstand their attack. She set up vipers and dragons, and the monster LAHAMU. And hurricanes, and raging hounds, and scorpion-men, And mighty tempests, and fish-men, and rams; They bore cruel weapons, without fear of the fight. Her commands were mighty, none could resist them; After this fashion she made eleven kinds of monsters.

Among the gods who were her sons, Inasmuch as he had given her support, She exalted KINGU; in their midst she raised him to power. To march before the forces, to lead the host, To give the battle-signal, to advance to the attack, To direct the battle, to control the fight, Unto him she entrusted, saying: "I have uttered the spell, In the assembly of the gods I have raised thee to power. The dominion over all the gods, I have entrusted unto thee. Be thou exalted, you are my chosen spouse, May your name be magnified among all ANUN-NAKI."

She gave him the Tablets of Destiny, on his breast she laid them, Saying: "Thy command shall not be in vain, And your decrees shall be established." Now KINGU, thus exalted, having received the power of ANU, Decreed the fate among the gods his sons, Saying: "Let the opening of your mouth quench the Fire-god; He who is exalted in the battle, let him display his might!"

TABLET II

TIAMAT made weighty her handiwork, Evil she wrought against the gods her children. To avenge APSU, TIAMAT planned evil, But how she had collected her forces, the god unto EA [ENKI] divulged. ENKI was grievously afflicted and he sat in sorrow.

The days went by, and his anger was appeased, And to the place of ANSAR his father he took his way. He went and, standing before ANSAR, his father, All that TIAMAT had plotted he repeated unto him, saying "TIAMAT, our mother hath conceived a hatred for us; With all her force she rages, full of wrath. All the gods have turned to her; With those, whom you created, they go to her side.

They have banded together and at the side of TIAMAT; And they advance; they are furious, They devise mischief without resting night and day. They prepare for battle, fuming and raging; They have joined their forces and are making war. TIAMAT, who formed all things, And made weapons invincible;

She hath spawned monster-serpents, Sharp of tooth, and merciless of fang. With poison, instead of blood, she hath filled their bodies. Fierce monster-vipers she hath clothed with terror; With splendor she has armed them; She has made them tall in stature. Whoever beholds them is overcome by terror, Their bodies rear up and none can withstand their attack.

She hath set up vipers, and dragons, and the monster LAHAMU; And hurricanes and raging hounds, and scorpion-men; And mighty tempests, and fish-men and rams; They bear cruel weapons, without fear of the fight. Her commands are mighty; none can resist them; After this fashion, huge of stature, She has made eleven kinds of monsters. Among the gods who are her sons, Inasmuch as he has given her support, She has exalted KINGU; In their midst she hath raised him to power.

To march before the forces, to lead the host, To give the battle-signal, to advance to the attack. To direct the battle, to control the fight, To him she has uttered the spell; She hath given to him the Tablets of Destiny, On his breast she laid them, saying: 'Thy command shall not be in vain; And your word shall be established.' "O my father, let not the word of thy lips be overcome, Let me go, that I may accomplish all that is in thy heart. I shall avenge."

TABLET III

ANSAR spoke to his minister: "O GAGA, thou minister who causes my spirit to rejoice; Unto LAHMU and LAHAMU I will send thee. Make ready for a feast, at a banquet let them sit, Let them eat bread, let them mix wine, That for MARDUK, the avenger, they may decree the fate. Go, GAGA, stand before them, And all that I tell thee, Repeat unto them, and say: 'ANSAR, your son, has sent me, The purpose of his heart he has made known unto me.

He said that TIAMAT, our mother, has conceived a hatred for us; With all her force she rages full of wrath. All the gods have turned to her, with those, whom you created; They go to her side. I sent ANU, but he could not withstand her; NUDIM-MUD [ENKI] was afraid and turned back. But MARDUK has set out, the champion of the gods, your son; To set out against TIAMAT his heart has called him. He opened his mouth and spake unto me, Saying: 'If I, your avenger, Conquer TIAMAT and give you life, appoint an assembly, make my fate preeminent and proclaim it so. In UP-SUKKINAKU seat yourself joyfully together; With my word in place I will decree fate. May whatsoever I do remain unaltered, May the word of my lips never be changed nor made of no avail.' Quickly decree for him the fate which you bestow So that he may go and fight your strong enemy."

GAGA went humbly before LAHMU and LA-HAMU, the gods, his fathers, and he kissed the ground at their feet. He humbled himself; then he stood up and spake unto them saying: "ANSAR, your son, has sent me; The purpose of his heart he hath made known unto me. He says that TIAMAT, our mother, hath conceived a hatred for us; With all her force she rages full of wrath." And he spoke the words of the tale. LAHMU and LAHAMU heard and cried aloud. All of the IGIGI wailed bitterly, saying: "We do not understand the deed of TIAMAT!"

Then did they collect and go—The Great Gods, all of them, the ANUNNAKI who decree fate. They entered in the House of ANSAR, kissed one another, They made ready for the feast, ate bread; And they mixed sesame-wine. They were wholly at ease, their spirit was exalted; Then for MARDUK, their avenger, they decreed the fate.

TABLET IV

The ANUNNAKI prepared for MARDUK a lordly chamber; Before his fathers as prince he took his place. "MARDUK, You are now chief among the Great Gods, Thy fate is unequaled, thy word is ANU. Your words shall be command, In your power shall it be to exalt and to abase. None among the gods shall transgress your boundary. Abundance, shall exist in thy sanctuary shrine, Even if you lack offerings. MARDUK, you are our avenger! We give you sovereignty over the whole world. Sit down in might; be exalted in thy command. Your weapon shall never lose its power; it shall crush your enemy. Lord, spare the life of him that puts his trust in thee; But as for the god who began the rebellion, empty them of life."

The ANUNNAKI set out a garment and continued to speak to MARDUK: "May thy fate, O lord, be supreme among the gods; To destroy and to create; speak only the word; And your command shall be fulfilled. Command now that the garment vanish; And speak the word again and let the garment re-appear!" Then he spake the words and the garment vanished; Again he commanded it and the garment reappeared.

When the gods, his fathers, beheld the fulfillment of his word; They rejoiced, and they did homage unto him, saying, "Maerdechai! Maerdechai! MARDUK is king!" They bestowed upon him the scepter, the throne and the ring; They gave him invincible weaponry to overwhelm the enemy. "Go, and cut off the life of TIAMAT," they said. "And let the wind carry her blood into secret places."

MARDUK made ready the bow, his first choice in weapon; He slung a spear upon him. He raised the club in his right hand. The bow and the quiver he hung at his side. He set the FLAMING DISC in front of him; And with the flame he filled his body. He fashioned a net to enclose the inward parts of TIAMAT, He stationed the four winds so that nothing of her might escape; The South wind and the North wind and the East wind; And the West wind He created the evil wind; And the tempest, and the hurricane; And the fourfold wind; And the sevenfold wind, and the cyclone; And the wind which had no equal; He sent forth the winds which he had created, seven in total; To disturb the inward parts of TIAMAT.

Then MARDUK raised the thunderbolt, mounted the chariot; A storm unequaled for terror, and he harnessed four horses named DESTRUCTION, FEROCITY, TERROR, and SWIFTNESS; and foam came from their mouths; And they were mighty in battle, trained to trample underfoot.

With garments cloaked in terror and an over-powering brightness crowning his head, MAR-DUK set out toward the raging TIAMAT. Then the gods beheld him. And when the lord drew near, He gazed upon the inward parts of TIAMAT, He heard the muttering of KINGU, her spouse.

As MARDUK gazed, KINGU was troubled; The will of KINGU was destroyed and his motions ceased. And the gods, his helpers, who marched by his side, beheld their leader's fear and their sight was troubled. But TIAMAT did not turn her neck. She spit rebellious words.

MARDUK raised the thunderbolt; his mighty weapon, against TIAMAT, who was raging, and he called out: "You have become great as you have exalted yourself on high; And your heart has prompted you to call to battle. You have raised KINGU to be your spouse; You have chosen Evil and sinned against ANU and his decree. And against the gods, my fathers, you have dedicated yourself to a wicked plan. Let us face off now then in battle!"

When TIAMAT heard these words; She acted possessed and lost her sense of reason. She screamed wild, piercing cries; She trembled and shook to her very foundations. She recited an incantation, and cast a spell, And the gods of the battle cried out for their weapons.

Then TIAMAT and MARDUK advanced towards one another; The battle drew near.

Lord MARDUK spread out his net and caught her, And the evil wind that gathered behind him he let loose in her face when she opened her mouth fully. The terrible winds filled her belly; And her courage was taken from her; And her mouth opened wider.

MARDUK seized the spear and burst her belly; Severing her inward parts, he pierced her heart. He overcame her and cut off her life; He cast down her body and stood upon it. And after slaying TIAMAT, the leader of the ANCIENT ONES, The might was broken and her minions scattered. But they were surrounded, so that they could not escape.

MARDUK took them captive and broke their weapons; In the net they were caught and in the snare they sat down. And on the eleven monsters which she had filled with the power of striking terror, he brought them affliction; Their strength he stole and their opposition he trampled under his feet. From KINGU who he had conquered; He rightly took the Tablets of Destiny and sealed them with his seal, then hung them from his neck. Now after MARDUK had conquered and cast down his enemies; And had fully established ANSAR's triumph over the enemy; And had attained the purpose of NUDIMMUD [EA (ENKI)]; Over the captive gods he strengthened his position, and he returned to the conquered TIAMAT. With his merciless club he smashed her skull. He cut through the channels of her blood; And he made the North wind steal it away Outside in secret places between spaces. His fathers beheld, and rejoiced and were glad; Presents and gifts they brought unto him.

Then Lord MARDUK rested, gazing upon her dead body and devised a cunning plan. He split her up like a flat fish into two halves; One half of her he established a covering for heaven. Sealed with a GATE he stationed a WATCHER IAK SAKKAK and fixed him not to let her waters to ever come forth.

MARDUK passed through and surveyed the regions of Heaven; And over the Deep he set the dwelling of NUDIMMUD [ENKI]. And after measuring the structure of the Deep, he founded his Mansion, which was created likened to Heaven and he set down the fixed districts for ANU, EN-LIL and ENKI to reign.

TABLET V

MARDUK fixed the Star Gates of the Elder Gods;[7] And the stars he gave images as the stars of the Zodiac, which he fixed in place. He ordained the year and into sections he divided it; For the twelve months he fixed the stars.

He founded his Star Gate on NIBIRU[8] to fix them in zones; That none might rebel or go astray, he fixed the Star Gate of ENLIL[9] and IA [ENKI] alongside him. He opened great gates on both sides; He made strong gates on the left and on the right and in the midst thereof he fixed the zenith; He fixed the Star Gate for the Moon-god and decreed that he shine forth, trusting him with the night and to determine days; The first of the great gates he assigned to NANNA [SIN] and every month without ceasing he would be crowned, Saying: "At the beginning of the month, when you shine down upon the land, you command the trumpets of the six days of the moon, and on the seventh day you will divide the crown. On the

---

7 Presumably the formation of the local universe (solar system) of planets.

8 Interpreted by some scholars as the planet Jupiter.

9 ENLIL —listed as BEL in many versions.

fourteenth day you will stand opposite as half-moon. When the Sun-god of the foundation of heaven calls thee; On that the final day again you will stand as opposite. All shall go about the course I fix. You will be drawn near to judge the righteous and destroy the unrighteous. That is my decree and the covenant of the first gate."

The gods, his fathers, beheld the net which MARDUK had fashioned; They beheld his bow and how its work was accomplished. They praised the work which he had done and then ANU raised up and kissed the bow before the assembly of the gods. And thus he named the names of the bow, saying: "Long-wood shall be one name; And the second name shall be Dragonslayer, And its third name shall be the Bow-star, in heaven shall it remain as a sign to all."

Then ANU and MARDUK fixed a Star Gate for it too; And after the ANUNNAKI decreed the fates for the ANCIENT ONES, MARDUK set a throne in heaven for himself at ANU's right hand.

TABLET VI

The ANUNNAKI acclaimed him "First among the ELDER GODS." MARDUK heard the praises of the gods; His heart called to him to devise a cunning plan. He approached IA [ENKI] saying: "The Key to the GATE shall be ever hidden, except to my offspring. I will take my blood and with bone I will fashion a Race of Men, that they may keep watch over the GATE. And from the blood of KINGU I will create a race of men, that they will inhabit the Earth in service to the gods so that our shrines may be built and the temples filled. But I will alter the ways of the gods, and I will change their paths; Together shall they be oppressed and unto evil shall they no longer reign. I will bind the ELDER GODS to the WATCHTOWERS; let them keep watch over the GATE of ABSU and the GATE of TI.AM.TU and the GATE of KINGU. I bind the WATCHER IAK SAKKAK to the GATE with the Key known only to my Race. Let none enter that GATE; Since to invoke DEATH is to utter the final prayer."

The ANUNNAKI rejoiced and set their mansions in UPSUKKINAKU. When all this had been done, the Elders of the ANUNNAKI seated themselves around MARDUK and in their assembly they exalted him and named him FIFTY times, bestowing upon him the FIFTY powers of the gods.

THE TABLET OF THE FIFTY NAMES

1. The First Name is MARDUK-DUGGA-ANU, Son of the Sun, Lord of Lords, Master of Magicians; Most Radiant Among the Gods is he.

2. The Second Name is MARDUKKA, ANUNNAKI Creator, Knower of the Secrets of MAR-

DUK, Time, Space & Creation [Geometry of the Universe].

3. The Third Name is ARRA-MARUTUKKU, Master of Protections and of the Gate to the AN-CIENT ONES; And to whom the people give praise as Protector of the City. Possessor of the ARRA-Star.

4. The Fourth Name is BARASHAKUSHU-BAALDURU, Worker of Miracles, with wide heart and strong sympathies.

5. The Fifth Name is LUGGAL-DIMMERANKI-BANUTUKKU, Commander of the Wind Demons, The Voice Heard Among the Gods.

6. The Sixth Name is NARI-LUGGAL-DIMM-ERANKI(A)-BAN-RABISHU, Watcher of the Star Gates of the IGIGI & ANUNNAKI; And who is named the Monitor of the Gods in their stations. Keeper of the Gates between worlds.

7. The Seventh Name is ASARU-LUDU-BAN-MASKIM, Wielder of the Flaming Sword, The Light of the Gods. Called for the safety and protection of the Gatekeeper.

8. The Eighth Name is NAMTILLAKU-BAN-UTUK-UKUT-UKKU, Master of the Death Gate and of Necromancy; And who is able to revive the Gods with a single prayer.

9. The Ninth Name is NAMRU-BAKA-KAL-

AMU, The Shining One who is Counselor of the Sciences. Called to increase the scientific knowledge of the Gatekeeper.

10. The Tenth Name is ASARU-BAALPRIKU, Creator of grains and plants, who knows no wasteland. Called to increase the vegetative and blooming growth.

11. The Eleventh Name is ASARU-ALIM-BAR-MARATU, who is revered for wisdom in the house of counsel; And who is looked to for peace when the Gods are unsettled. Called to aid in communication with the ANUNNAKI and to dispel deception.

12. The Twelfth Name is ASARU-ALIM-NUNA-BANA-TATU, The Mighty One who is the Light of the Father of the Gods; And who directs the decrees of ANU, ENLIL and ENKI/EA. Called to aid in the enforcement of law on Earth.

13. The Thirteenth Name is (NABU)-TUTU, He who created them anew, and should their wants be pure, then they are satisfied. Called to reveal the hidden gnosis within the Gatekeeper.

14. The Fourteenth Name is ZI-UKKINA-GIBIL-ANU, The life of the Assembly of the Gods; Who established for a bright place for the Gods in the heavens. Called to reveal the secrets of astrology and the celestial sphere.

15. The Fifteenth Name is ZI-AZAG-ZI-KU-

IGIGI-MAGAN-PA, Bringer of Purification, God of the Favoring Breeze, Carrier of Wealth & Abundance to the people.

16. The Sixteenth Name is AGAKU-AZAG-MASH-GARZANNA, Lord of the Pure Incantation, The Merciful One; And whose name is on the mouth of the Created Race. Called to bring life to elementaries and ward spirits.

17. The Seventeenth Name is TUKUMU-AZAG-MASH-SHAMMASHTI, Knower of the Incantation to destroy all evil ones. Called in the Maqlu Rite to dispel evil sorceries.

18. The Eighteenth Name is SAHG-ZU-MASH-SHANANNA, Founder of the Assembly of Gods and knows their heart; And whose name is heralded among the IGIGI. Called for aiding the Gatekeepers psychic development.

19. The Nineteenth Name is ZI-SI-MASH-IN-ANNA, Reconciler of enemies, who puts an end to anger; Bringer of Peace.

20. The Twentieth Name is SUH-RIM-MASH-SHA-NERGAL, Destroyer of wicked foes, who confuses their plans. May be sent to destroy the enemies of the Gatekeeper.

21. The Twenty-first Name is SUH-KUR-RIM-MASH-SHADAR, Who confounds the wicked foes in their places. May be sent to destroy the unknown enemies of the Gatekeeper.

22. The Twenty-second Name is ZAH-RIM-MASH-SHAG-ARANNU, Lord of Lightning, A warrior among warriors. May be raised against entire armies of men.

23. The Twenty-third Name is ZAH-KUR-RIM-MASH-TI-SHADDU, Destroyer of the Enemy in battle; Who slays in a most unnatural fashion.

24. The Twenty-fourth Name is ENBILULU-MASH-SHA-NEBU, Knower of the secrets of water and of secret places for grazing. Called to bestow the secrets of dowsing and aid irrigation.

25. The Twenty-fifth Name is EPADUN-E-YUNGINA-KANPA, Lord of Irrigation, who sprinkles water in the heavens and on Earth. As the previous, also the secrets of Sacred Geometry.

26. The Twenty-sixth Name is ENBI-LU-LU-GUGAL-AGGA, Lord of growth and cultivation, who raises the grains to maturity; And some have said is a face of ENKI.

27. The Twenty-seventh Name is HEGAL-BURDISHU, Master of farming and the plentiful harvest; And who provides for the people's consumption. May also be called to aid in personal fertility.

28. The Twenty-eighth Name is SIRSIR-APIRI-KUBAB-ADAZU-ZU-KANPA, The domination of TIAMAT by the power of the Net. Called for mastery of the Serpent and the Kundalini.

29. The Twenty-ninth Name is MAL-AHK-BACH-ACHA-DUGGA, Lord of bravery and courage, Rider of the Ancient Worm. Summoned for courage, bravery and self-confidence.

30. The Thirtieth Name is GIL-AGGA-BAAL, Furnisher of the life-giving seed, Beloved (betrothed) consort to INANNA-ISHTAR. Called for women who desire pregnancy.

31. The Thirty-first Name is GILMA-AKKA-BAAL, Mighty One and Divine Architect of the temples. Possesses secrets concerning the Geometry of the Universe.

32. The Thirty-second Name is AGILMA-MASH-SHAY-E-GURRA, Maker of Rain Clouds to nourish the fields of the Earth. Called forth in times of drought.

33. The Thirty-third Name is ZULUM-MU-AB-BA-BAAL, Giver of excellent counsel and power in all businesses; And Destroyer of the wicked foe, maintaining goodness and order.

34. The Thirty-fourth Name is MUMMU, Creator of the Universe from the flesh of TI.AM.TU. Keeper of the Four Watchtower Gates to the Outside.

35. The Thirty-fifth Name is ZU-MUL-IL-MAR-AN-DARA-BAAL; The heavens have none equal in strength and vitality. Called forth to aid in healing rituals and rites.

36. The Thirty-sixth Name is AGISKUL-AG-NI-BAAL-LUGAL-ABDUBAR, Who sealed the ANCIENT ONES in the abyss. Called by the piously righteous for strength and vigor.

37. The Thirty-seventh Name is PAGALGUEN-NA-ARRA-BA-BAAL, Possessor of Infinite Intelligence, preeminent among the Gods. Offers wisdom in oracles and divination.

38. The Thirty-eighth Name is LUGAL-DUR-MAH-ARATA-AGAR-BAAL, King of the gods, Lord of Rulers [*durmah*]. Aids the Gatekeeper in developing all mystic powers.

39. The Thirty-ninth Name is ARRA-ADU-NUNA-ARAMAN-GI, Counselor of ENKI/EA, who created the Gods, his fathers; And whose princely ways no other God can equal. Called during (self)-initiations to aid you through the Gates.

40. The Fortieth Name is DUL-AZAG-DUMU-DUKU-ARATA-GIGI, Possessor of the secret knowledge and the wand of Lapis Lazuli. Can reveal untold marvels of the cosmos to the Gatekeeper.

41. The Forty-first Name is LUGAL-AB-BA-BAAL-DIKU, Eldest of the Elder Ones, and pure is his dwelling among them. Aids the Gatekeeper in acquiring "Self-Honesty."

42. The Forty-second Name is LUGALDUL-AZAGA-ZI-KUR, Knower of the secrets of the spirits of wind and star. Offers the Gatekeeper secrets to command the spirits.

43. The Forty-third Name is IR-KINGU-BAR-E-RIMU, Holding the capture of KINGU, supreme is his might. Keeper of the Blood(Birth)-Rights.

44. The Forty-fourth Name is KI-EN-MA-EN-GAIGAI, Supreme Judge of the ANUNNAKI, at whose name the gods quake. To be called when no other spirit will arrive.

45. The Forty-fifth Name is E-ZIS-KUR-NEN-IGEGAI, Knows the lifespan of all things; And who fixed the Created Race's life at 120 years.

46. The Forty-sixth Name is GIBIL-GIRRA-BAAL-AGNI-TARRA, Lord of the sacred fire and the forge, creator of the Sword. Also possesses the secrets of the "fiery passions."

47. The Forty-seventh Name is ADDU-KAKO-DAMMU, Raiser of storms that blanket the skies of Heaven.

48. The Forty-eighth Name is ASH-ARRU-BAX-TAN-DABAL, Keeper of time, the secrets of the past and future. May be summoned to aid acts of divination.

49. The Forty-ninth Name is The STAR, let NE-BIRU be his name; He who forced his way through the midst of TIAMAT, May he hold the ALPHA and the OMEGA in his hands. Summoned to discern the Destiny of the Universe.

50. The Fiftieth Name is FIFTY and NINNU-AM-GASHDIG, The Judger of Judges, Determiner of the laws of the Realm. The Patron of the Dragonblood Kings of Earth.

THE MARDUK TABLET APOCRYPHA

The Forty-ninth Name is the STAR, that which shines in the heavens. May he hold the ALPHA and the OMEGA in his hands; And may all pay homage unto him, saying: "He who forced his way through the midst of TI.AM.TU without resting, Let NIBIRU be his name – The Seizer of the Crossings[10] that causes the stars of heaven to uphold their paths. He comes as a shepherd to the gods who are like sheep. In the future of mankind at the End of Days, may this be heard without ceasing; may it hold sway forever! Since MARDUK created the realm of heaven and fashioned the firm earth, He is forever the Lord of this World."

ENLIL listened. ENKI heard and rejoiced. All of the Spirits of Heaven waited. ENLIL gave to MARDUK his name and title BEL. ENKI gave to MARDUK his name and title EA and said: "The binding of all my decrees, let MARDUK now control. All of my commands, shall he make known."

The Fiftieth Name is FIFTY and NINNU-AM-GASHDIG, The Judger of Judges, Determiner of the laws of the Realm. By the name FIFTY did the ANUNNAKI then proclaim MARDUK's "Fifty

---

10 NIBIRU —given as *"Nebiru"* in some translations, meaning literally "Crossings" such as "in or around a midsection" or "midway around."

Names." The ANUNNAKI made his path preeminent.

Let the Fifty Names of MARDUK be held in remembrance to all; And let the leaders proclaim them; Let the wise gather to consider them together; Let the father repeat them and teach them to his son; Let them be in the ears of the priest and the shepherd. Let all men rejoice in MARDUK, the Lord of the gods,

That he may cause the land, his Earth, to be prosperous; And that he himself may enjoy prosperity! His word holds and his command is unaltered; No utterance from his mouth goes unnoticed. His gaze is of anger and turns his back to none; No god can withstand his wrath. And yet, wide is his heart and broad is his compassion; The sinner and evil-doer in his presence weep for themselves and pray for forgiveness.

DICTIONARY OF ANUNNAKI GODS

ADAD {10}—The youngest son of ENLIL that becomes the national patron deity to the *Hittites* (called HADAD or TESHUB); possibly also recognized as BAAL HADAD in a *Hittite* version of the Supernal Trinity that is elevated to a chief god position in the same manner that MARDUK is raised in *Babylon*. As a storm god in the Anunnaki pantheon, ADAD is represented by thunder, lightning and torrents. According to Hittite records, succession of hierarchical kingship passes from ALALU to ANU to KUMARBI (ENLIL) and then BA'AL HADAD (TESHUB). In the Enki'ite (Mardukite) Babylonian system he is named ISHKUR and granted the position of *"Inspector of the Cosmos"* by ENKI.

ALALU [*"Father of the Gods"*]—The figure maintaining 'kingship' in the 'heavens' prior to ANU. An ancient *Hittite (Hurrian)* tablet cycle titled ALALU & ANU or *"Kingship in Heaven"* describes a conflict between the two for the seat of 'kingship' in the 'heavens'. The Mardukite *Tablet-K* series reprinted in *"The Anunnaki Bible"* explains: Formerly in the Ancient of Days, ALULU was reigning in heaven; and for nine *sars* did he rule the skies, but not well did he reign. Then in the ninth *sar* of his reign, ANU defeated ALULU. ALULU descended from heaven and ruled the dark-hued earth. ANU gave fight and defeated

ALULU and kingship was lowered from heaven to earth by decree of ANU.

ALULU *see* ALALU

ASAR(I)LUHI *see* MARDUK

AMARUTU *see* MARDUK

AN/ANSAR *see* ANU

ANTU {55} ["*Life of Heaven*"]—The official half-sister (by a different mother) and spouse (consort) of ANU. ANTU and ANU beget ENLIL. In archaic pre-*Sumerian* lore, ANTU is espoused to the archaic AN.

ANUNITUM *see* INANNA

ANU {60} ["*Heavenly One*"]—In the *Sumerian* Anunnaki pantheon, ANU is the supreme "*All-Father*" of the pantheon; father to ENLIL by official spouse ANTU, and the father of ENKI & NINHURSAG (by other wives). Called AN in pre-*Babylonian* times and ANU by the *Babylonians*, a being whose family resides on, or emerged from the 'place of crossings' (*Nibiru*). Few of the incantation tablets (or 'prayers') invoke the powers of ANU directly, since the "heavenly force" was perceived as too vast to be channeled in its raw state, and to degrade it to anything more accessible would be to compromise the nature of what is being represented by this figure.

ANZU ["*Knower of Heaven*"]—An obscure bird-like beast/monster of an unclear nature. The ANZU or ZU usually refers to a "heavenly bird" or thunderbird that appears in an archaic tab-let cycle stealing the '*Tablets of Destiny*" from EN-LIL, disrupting the DUR-AN-KI ('Bond-Heav-en-Earth') "stargate." It is possible that this half-man, half-bird, sometimes called AZAG, was a ge-netically engineered storm-god or artificially intel-ligent messenger being of ENLIL that turned "evil."

ARURU—The sister of ENLIL, alias NINTU, who is the *Babylonian* title for the 'mother-god-dess' known in *Sumerian* as NINMAH or NIN-HURSAG. In the Babylonian ethnocentric epics, she assists MARDUK in creating the human race (or '*Race of Marduk*'), however, in the *Enuma Elis*, it is "blood" of KINGU that is used. Other *Sumerian* versions say the "blood" or "essence" of some other 'slain' god is used for this.

AYA ["*Dawn*"]—The official spouse (consort) of SAMAS in *Akkadian*; named SHERIDA in *Sumerian*.

AZAG *see* ANZU

BAU ["*To Accompany*"]—A daughter of ANU, who is the official spouse (consort) to NINURTA in the pre-*Babylonian* (*Sumerian*) pantheon. Her names GULA ("*Big One*") and BAU (the sound a dog makes) are, perhaps idioms about her size/appearance. She remains a goddess in the *Babylonian* pantheon of healing (as NINTI-NUGGA).

BEL *see* EL

BUZUR *see* ENKI

DAMKINA *see* NINKI

DAMUZU *see* DUMUZI

DUMUZI ["*Son Who is Life*"]—Youngest son of ENKI and DUTTUR (a concubine of ENKI) who is the betrothed spouse (consort) to INANNA (ISHTAR) after MARDUK declines the tradition of espousing INANNA. DAMUZI is a shepherd god (as opposed to a grain deity), known as TAMMUZ in the Semitic languages. In the *Sumerian* version of the descent-cycle, INANNA descends to the *Underworld* in hopes of being its queen. When captured, she becomes a prisoner of her sister ERESHKIGAL and leaves to find someone to take her place. Upon returning to ERECH, she finds that DUMUZI has been celebrating his ascent to her throne and is not mourning for her death. Enraged, she immediately hands him over to the 'demons' of the *Underworld*. Later versions of this cycle depict the god MARDUK as somehow responsible for the death of DUMUZI and INANNA (ISHTAR) descends to the *Underworld* to release him.

EA *see* ENKI

EL—A Semitic form of the Akkadian (*Babyloni-an*) ILU or ILI, meaning '*Lofty Ones*', '*High Ones*' or '*Great Gods*'; the plural form being ILANI (or ELANI in *European Elvish-Faerie* lore), with a Semitic plural equivalent "*Elohim*", meaning literally 'gods' but often used to denote the 'One God' in the Judeo-Christian *Old Testament* (which is, itself, rooted strongly in Mesopotamian traditions). EL or BEL is also used to denote the 'Lord of the Earth-Space', or else 'ENLIL-SHIP', a position attributed not only to ENLIL (in the *Enlilite Sumerian* tradition) but also to NINURTA, MAR-DUK and even other patron deities by localized Middle Eastern cults. Later Semitic use of EL as a suffix (e.g., Micha*el*, Gabri*el*, etc.) matches the prefix use of the ILU sign in cuneiform, meaning "*Of God.*" In cuneiform, the sign is a "cross" and in later religious scriptures and rites, the literary tradition remained to place a cross before a *Divine* or saint name.

ELLIL *see* ENLIL

ENKI {40} "*Lord of the Earth*"—also known as E.A. ["*Whose Home is Water*"], firstborn son of ANU (but not the official heir), half-brother to ENLIL (heir of ANU). Also called NUDIMMUD (or PTAH in *Egypt*) meaning: "*The Fashioner*" (or "*Grand Designer*"). ENKI is the Chief scientist of the Anunnaki, taking up residence in *Eridu*, near the *Persian Gulf* and also in *Africa* (particularly *Egypt*). ENKI is father of MARDUK, begot with NINKI (DAMKINA) and is representative of the planet Neptune in the local Anunnaki 'world order'. ENKI is given control of the *'Waters of Life'* on Earth. He seeks to save his own (*'Mardukite'*) legacy during the deluge and then is responsible for programing the arts and sciences of civilization into humanity. In later *Enlilite*-derived Judeo-Christian interpretations, ENKI becomes demonized as 'Satan'.

ENLIL {50} *"Lord of Air-Space"*—The official heir-son of ANU, *'Lord of the Command'* on Earth, revered as the *'God'* of Earth by Enlilite *Sumerians* and later derived Semitic (Hebrew) tradtions. EN-LIL begets his own heir, NINURTA, by his half-sister NINHURSAG, but espouses SUD, renamed NINLIL and begets NANNA. In the pre-*Babylonian* paradigm, ENLIL is the Jupiter position in the pantheon that is later usurped by MARDUK. *Sumerian* tradition observes ENLIL as the 'Father' to the Anunnaki pantheon, much in the same way that ENKI is revered by the *Mardukites*. Prominent descendents of ENLIL include: NANNA, SAMAS, INANNA and NERGAL in addition to NINURTA.

ENSAG *see* NABU

ENSHAG *see* NABU

ERESHKIGAL – [*"Mistress of the Great Below"*] The Queen of the *Great Lands* in the *Sumerian* tradition, sister of INANNA-ISHTAR, granddaughter of ENLIL and spouse to NERGAL.

ERRA *see* NERGAL

GANZIR — The gatekeeper to the underworld 'Kingdom of Shadows.' The *'Gate of Ganzir'* is often confused with the *'Gate to the Abyss'* or the *'Gate to the Outside'*, but instead it is a portal into the Anunnaki-controlled *Underworld*, the *'Shadowlands'* or twilight world within the domain of ERESHKIGAL, who rules this 'land of the dead'. Quoting a modern grimoire of Babylonian occultism, the "necromantic art, by which is it desirous to speak with the phantom of someone dead, and perhaps dwelling in the ABSU [*Abyss*] and thereby a servant of ERESHKIGAL... it is no less than the opening of the *Gate of Ganzir.*"

GIBIL [*"He Who Has Fire"*]—The companion of the flame, a descendent of ENKI who uses fire to conduct alchemy and other feats of *"fire power."*

GIRRA—The "servant", "power" or "fire" of the 'great god'; the *Sumerian* fire-god or essence or force of a fire-god named GIBIL.

GULA *see* BAU

HADAD *see* ADAD

ILLIL *see* ENLIL

ILU *see* EL

IMDUGUD *see* ANZU

INANNA {15} [*"Lady of Heaven"*]—The *Sumerian* goddess of "passion", both 'love' and 'war', and patron of URUK, begot by NANNA and NINGAL; originally betrothed to MARDUK, she then changes her consort choice to DUMUZI. Her prowess and determination secured her a place in all ancient pantheons; being the *"Goddess of One-Thousand Names,"* titled ISHTAR in *Babylon*. INANNA (ISHTAR) is the spirit of Venus, whose day is Friday and with an essence found in copper. Her colors are green and white, significant to her domain of fertility and growth. She offers her magicians the skills in love and visions of beauty.

IRRA *see* NERGAL

ISHKUR *see* ADAD

ISHTAR *see* INANNA

KUR *see* TIAMAT

MAMMI *see* NINHURSAG

MARDUK {10/(50)} *"Son of God"*—The supreme champion of the IGIGI during the pre-

Sumerian era of the Anunnaki; heir-son of ENKI, he becomes the patron of *Babylon* and the 'Mardukite' tradition reigning for the *Age of Aries* in Mesopotamia. All tablet cycles making reference to MARDUK are purely *Babylonian* or from a direct later source, as he does not appear in any significant pre-Babylonian cuneiform tablet cycles yet unearthed. When mentioned briefly as the son of ENKI, working in *Eridu*, he is named AS-ARLUHI, becoming the patron Anunnaki "deity" of magic or 'Master of Magicians'after having inherited the craft from his father. The blatant industrious and expansive power represented by MARDUK in his ascent up the pantheon (as observed in *Babylon*) is typified by the planet Jupiter (ENLIL, by *Sumerian* standards). His color is purple.

MERIDUG *see* MARDUK

MERODACH *see* MARDUK

NABAK *see* NABU

NABIH *see* NABU

NABU {12} ["*Prophet*"]—The official post-*Sumerian* secretary of the Anunnaki, part-divine earth born heir-son of MARDUK and messenger-herald and spokesperson of the '*Mardukite*' tradition, the national cult of *Babylon* devised by NABU who assisted his father in the redevelopment of the Anunnaki paradigm (as seen in the

158

'*Mardukite*' religion of *Babylon* replacing the previously observed '*Enlilite*' world order of the
Sumerians). Creating the concept of 'history' and
'propaganda', NABU gives the 'stylus' to humanity
(and launches a group of scribe-priests (specially
taught writing and rhetoric) to catalog the natures,
identities, history and decrees (decisions) of the
Anunnaki Assembly (gods) and their relationship
with each other and the human ("mortal") world,
thereby creating not only the first public 'religion',
but the first 'mythology' (a religion rooted in literary and oral legacies of human relationships and
encounters with the divine) and the systems that
were able to later result (most of which are still
functioning as part of 'normal' everyday life in
contemporary society). NABU is the archetypal
'*High Priest*' (ENSAG) of the first religion (dedicated to MARDUK) and practiced by priests who
preserve the craft of ENKI in *Eridu* with science
and 'magic' of the gods to power and sustain the
prosperous longevity of *Babylon*.

NAMRASIT *see* NANNA

NAMMTAR *see* NAMTAR

NAMMU *see* TIAMAT

NAMTAR ["*Fate Maker*"]—The 'Black Magi-
ci-an', vizier of ERESHKIGAL in the *Underworld*,
also likened to the *Assyrian (Chaldean)* plague-
god NAMTARU (also the *Akkadian* word for pest-

ilence"). From a ritual text given in *Liber 9* (Tablet-Q in *The Complete Anunnaki Bible*), the priest is to make an image of the affected (sick) person in dough [flour], so as to force the 'plague-god' that afflicts the person to come away from the body and go into the image. The ancient tablets list the name of the plague-god as NAMTARU, and in other places as URA and even URAS (in *Egypt*). In the 'Descent'-cycle, ERESHKIGAL summoned NAMMTAR, the Black Magician, saying these words as she spoke to him: 'Go, NAMMTAR, imprison her [INANNA] in Darkness, in my castle! Release against her the Seven Anunnaki Judges! Release against her the Demons of the Deep...' Then, finally, the representation of a 'demon', like the plague-god NAMTARU, was not intended for 'worship' or 'veneration' (as we might see glorified among today's misguided attempts toward 'dark paths') as a deity. Such statuary typically was constructed only to be 'ceremonially' annihilated or buried as a 'ward' against what the statue (deity) represented.

NAMTARU *see* NAMTAR

NANNA {30}—The official lunar deity of the Enlilite *Sumerian* Anunnaki pantheon, the moon-god, reigning with his feminine lunar consort, NINGAL. An Anunnaki designation of 30 is significant to the approximate number of days in a month; whereby the original Sumerian calendar consists of twelve cycles of 30 days for a 360 day year (and the reason a circle is divided into 360 degrees). NANNA and NINGAL begot the twins: INANNA and SAMAS; mythographically, the *moon* gave birth to the *sun* and *Venus* is a twin-star to the *sun*. To the ancient, the moon was the 'sun-at-night'. It illuminated the pathway for travelers and kept 'watch' as the people slept. Just as the sun is invoked to grant judgments of the daytime [see SAMAS], the moon is given domain of the night and *dreamscapes* (including the 'astral plane'). The day, "Monday", is obviously named after the moon, and is likewise sacred. The essence and color of silver is usually corresponded.

NANNAR *see* NANNA

NEBO *see* NABU

NERGAL {8}—The official spouse (consort) of ERESHKIGAL (*'Queen of the Underworld'*). NERGAL corresponds to the symbol and energetic current of *Mars,* with a fiery and destructive nature commemorated in the *Babylonian* epithet ERRA (*"Annihilator"*). The vitality and raw power of *Mars* (ruling Tuesday) is evident in the essences: iron and blood.

NINAGAL—An epithet meaning *"Prince of the Great Waters,"* the name appears for a son of ENKI, who in the *Ziusurda* (*Atra-Asis*) cycle is selected by ENKI to navigate the archetypal "ark" sea-craft during the Great Flood.

NINANNA *see* INANNA

NINGAL {25} [*"Great Lady"*]—The daughter of ENKI; espoused (consort) to NANNA (SIN) and the mother of INANNA (ISHTAR) and SAMAS.

NINGISHZIDA—The 'Lord of the Tree of Life', a son of ENKI and brother to MARDUK, known as *Hermes* and *Thoth-the-Elder* (or TUTU) in a time before NABU. He is a geneticist, trained under ENKI in the arts of life engineering (and reality engineering) that was later taught by NABU (*Thoth-the-Younger* or TUTU) and it evolved into the mystical school of 'Hermetics' (or 'Hermeticism'). Having lost in the 'Pyramid Wars' (c. 3400 B.C. to 3150 B.C.) against MARDUK (RA) and not participating in the pro-MARDUK revolution of ENKI's lineage, NINGISHZIDA establishes his own realm in South America, known by the indigenous people and tradition as QUETZAL-COATL, the 'feather-ed serpent' (literally 'plumed serpent').

NINHARSAG *see* NINHURSAG

NINHURSAG {5}—The chief Anunnaki physician, the mother of NINURTA by ENLIL; a half-sister to ENLIL and ENKI by ANU. In an attempt to produce a royal heir or his own, ENKI even courts her at one time. She is not espoused to any of the pantheon, but instead serves the role of 'birth-goddess' and 'midwife' to the birth and raising of the Anunnaki children (of the Younger Generation), carrying names like MAMMI (*"Mother"*) and NINTI (*"Lady of Life"*). When attempting to relieve the toiling of the IGIGI faction of the Anunnaki, ENKI seeks out NINHURSAG to assist in the 'creation' of the 'human' race. Her response, being: 'If ENKI will provide for me the clay, then I will make the creation'. In this antropogenetic cycle, she mixes the clay with the flesh and blood of 'Awmelu' (presumed to be a slain deity). In other versions, the 'essence' is more clearly semen and/or other genetic material. Cuneiform tablet records indicate that six different attempts are made before the '*Adamu*' (the seventh) is fashioned.

NINIB *see* NINURTA

NINKI {35} [*"Lady of the Earth"*]—The official spouse (consort) of ENKI, also known as DAMKINA [*"Lady Who Came to Earth"*]. NINKI is the daughter of ALALU (the 'heavenly' king prior to ANU) and the the mother of MARDUK.

NINLIL {45} *"Lady of Air-Space"*—The official spouse (consort) of ENLIL, also known with the epithet SUD ("nurse"). The background to the relationship between ENLIL and NINLIL is not commonly found in the typical cuneiform tablet cycles. Naturally, the lore is *not* Mardukite or

Babylonian in origin and does not appear in the tablet catalogue or commentary of (modern) Mardukite Core anthologies. The cycle is sometimes referred to as "*Enlil's Banishment to the Underworld.*"

NINMAH *see* NINHURSAG

NINSHUBAR *see* NINSHUBUR

NINSHUBUR ["*Lady of the East*"]—Personal assistant (Mercury), second-in-command to the goddess INANNA (ISHTAR). She does not take a consort and there is an alluded love-relationship between her and INANNA (ISHTAR).

NINSUBAR *see* NINSHUBUR

NINTI *see* NINHURSAG

NINTINUGGA *see* BAU

NINTU *see* ARURU

NINURTA {4/(50)} "*Lord of the South Wind*"— The official heir-son of ENLIL, born of ENLIL and NINMAH, espoused to BAU. NINURTA represents the current of Saturn in the Mardukite paradigm, representative both of "hidden power" and "hidden secrets" (an idiom for the dark power and secrets behind the origins and legacy of *Babylon*). In the Enlilite *Sumerian* worldview, NINURTA (called NINIB in *Babylonian*) is the

Enlil-in-waiting, a position usurped by MARDUK proper for the *Age of Aries*. As Enlilship is typically symbolized by 'dragon-slaying', the same motif present in the elevation of MARDUK in *Babylon* rivaling the dragon-queen TIAMAT can be seen in the older *Sumerian* cycles where the prowess of NINURTA is shown in his ability to fight the mighty dragon KUR. His colors are black and violet and his essence corresponds to the metal lead.

NIRGAL *see* NERGAL

NISABA—The *Sumerian* agricultural goddess of writing and scribes; replaced by the god NABU in the Mardukite *Babylonian* Anunnaki tradition.

NUDIMMUD *see* ENKI

NUNAMIR *see* ENLIL

NUSKU [*"Bringer of Light"*]—ENLIL's vizier.

NUZKU *see* NUSKU

OANNES *see* ENKI

RAMMAN(U) *see* ADAD

SAMAS {20}—The official solar deity of the Enlilite *Sumerian* Anunnaki pantheon, brother to INANNA (SHTAR), born of NANNA and NINGAL. The sun represents the brilliance and radiant energy of life on earth; the light that allows organic life to grow and even the manner of which 'time' [and 'lifespan'] is divided. Expansive powerful energy of the solar current is invoked in magical ceremonies for general success and well-being. The fiery nature of the 'star' is called upon to 'incinerate iniquities' and reveal the nature of darkness and lies, meaning: the revelation of truth. Mistaken (by modern scholars) as monotheistic 'sun worship', solar veneration is really the celebration of life. As an archetypal representative of the 'starry' 'heavens', the sun signifies a presence and watchful eye of the 'All-Seeing-God', invoked in matters of law to bring righteous judgment. Sunday is sacred to SAMAS along with the color yellow, and both the color and essence of gold.

SARPANIT {(5)/(45)}—Seventh generation of ADAPA (by ENKI), the chosen royal spouse (consort) of MARDUK; princess-queen patron goddess (ISHTAR) of *Babylon* and mother to NABU. In alternative versions of the lore, her name ERU (or ERUA) designates her as the 'mother-goddess' of the '*Children of MARDUK*' (later associated with the light-folk or elves of Europe).

SHAMMASH *see* SAMAS

SHERIDA *see* AYA

SIN *see* NANNA

SUD *see* NINLIL

166

SUEN *see* NANNA

TAMMUZ *see* DUMUZI

TEHOM *see* TIAMAT

TIAMAT [*"Life-Giving Mother"*]—The 'primeval dragon' in *Babylonian* archaic epics, often equated with the *Sumerian* KUR. Later esoteric traditions associate 'her' as *Yaldabaoth* (*Ialda-baoth*) in Gnostic Hermeticism, or *Khornozon* (*Choronzon*) in Enochian Hermeticism. She is equated with the 'waters' or the 'Deep' in post-Sumerian Semitic scripture (Hebrew: *tehom*) – the all-encompassing "Sea" is parted to reveal the first 'division' (fragmentation) of "Life" in the Universe. She is paired anthropomorphically with ABZU (the *Abyss*) as the prehistoric 'ancestors' of the Anunnaki race. Her primary literary presence as TIAMAT (or T(I)AMTU) is in the *Enuma Elis* (*Babylonian*) 'Epic of Creation'. In later times, the name is used for the wife of ADAMU (*Adam*), being the equivalent to the Semitic "Eve" character.

TUTU *see* NABU

UDDU/UTTU *see* SAMAS

ZARPANITUM *see* SARPANIT

SYS✦EMOLOGY

The Pathway to Self-Honesty

THE WAY INTO THE
FUTURE

A HANDBOOK FOR THE NEW HUMAN

JOSHUA FREE

THE WAY INTO THE
FUTURE

A Handbook for the New Human

A collection of writings by
Joshua Free
as selected by James Thomas

now available as a
Collector's Edition Hardcover

Here are the basic answers to what has held
Humanity back from achieving its ultimate
goals and unlocking true power of the Spirit
and the highest state of Knowing and Being.

"*The Way Into The Future*" illuminates the
Pathway leading to Planet Earth's true
"metahuman" destiny. With *excerpts from*
"*Tablets of Destiny*," "*Crystal Clear*,"
"*Systemology—The Original Thesis*" and
"*The Power of Zu*." You can help shine clear
light on anyone's pathway!

Carefully selected by Mardukite
Publications Officer, James Thomas,
this critical *collection of eighteen*
articles, lecture transcripts and reference
chapters by Joshua Free is sure to be
not only a treasured part
of your personal library,
but also the perfect gift—
an introduction to Systemology
for all friends, family and loved ones.

(*Basic Grade-III Introductory Pocket Anthology*)

SYSTEMOLOGY
The Pathway to Self-Honesty

GO FURTHER AND BE

CRYSTAL CLEAR

CRYSTAL CLEAR

(Handbook for Seekers)

Mardukite Systemology Liber-2B
by Joshua Free

now available as a
Revised Academy Edition Hardcover

Take control of your destiny
and chart the first steps
toward your own spiritual evolution.
Realize new potentials of the
Human Condition with
a Self-guiding handbook for
Self-Processing toward
Self-Actualization
in Self-Honesty using actual
techniques and training
provided for the coveted
"Mardukite Systemology Grade-III
Self-Defragmentation Course Program"
—once only available
directly and privately from
the underground Systemology Society.

Discover the amazing power behind the
applied spiritual technology
used for counseling and advisement in
the tradition of Mardukite Zuism.

PUBLISHED BY THE **JOSHUA FREE** IMPRINT REPRESENTING

The Founding Church of Mardukite Zuism

THE JOSHUA FREE IMPRINT
JFI PUBLICATIONS

MARDUKITE
ZUISM

mardukite.com